Where Are We Running?

Where Are We Running?

By June Strong

Southern Publishing Association, Nashville, Tennessee

Copyright © 1979 by
Southern Publishing Association

This book was
Designed by Mark O'Connor
Cover design by Steven Hall

Type set: 11/13 Times Roman

Printed in U.S.A.

Library of Congress Cataloging in Publication Data

Strong, June
   Where are we running?

   1. Christian life—Seventh-day Adventist authors.
I. Title.
BV4501.2.S818   248'.4   78-26271
ISBN 0-8127-0207-7

Acknowledgment

Appreciation to *These Times,* nationally acclaimed award-winning Christian journal, for permission to reprint the material that first appeared in their columns.

Contents

Where Are We Running?

"Be still and know that I am God" (Psalm 46:10).

Often in the early evening as low sun sprawls golden-soft across the wheat fields, my daughters and I bicycle down a little-traveled country road. Our progress is slow, for we stop to watch a plain brown mother duck lead her little ones across a farm pond, then again we gather feathery parasols of Queen Anne's lace.

Sometimes the girls wheel on ahead, and I have opportunity to thank God specifically for the undulating green carpet of oats on my right, the bell-tinkling sheep on my left. I never feel closer to Him than during those quiet miles at day's end.

Not far across the intervening fields lies a superhighway, I-90, and as we pedal leisurely along we can watch the snarling stream of tractor trailers, cars, campers, and motor homes—hurrying, hurrying, either toward or away from something. Vacationers seeking vistas better than they left behind. Truckers gobbling up the countryside with only their destination in mind.

The contrast molds my ponderings into a question

9

mark. Where are we running, we Americans? For I've been on the superhighway as well as on the country lane. I've held the speedometer on fifty-five, hour after hour, to reach a lonely motel and order a mediocre meal from a harried waitress.

Suddenly I want to flag them down, to holler stop, to march them all across the fields and show them God written in daisies around a soft-eyed newborn calf.

But they don't hear me. The tires just sing, "Hurry, hurry, hurry!" against the asphalt, and the people don't look left or right.

Why Wouldn't He Help Her?

I was entering our small white church on some week-day errand when I noted a strange scene at the busy intersection only a short distance away. There was a girl stumbling uncertainly about in an attempt to cross the street. The white cane with which she tapped her way along identified her as a student from the local school for the blind.

She waited, listening for the signal sound of moving traffic, then moved out to cross the busy highway. She had only to walk straight ahead, but how does one achieve "straight" without the luxury of vision? She angled frighteningly to the left, directly toward the path of fast-moving traffic, and a useless cry rose to my lips. She stopped. Not because of my warning—I was too far re-moved from the scene to be of any value—but because her ears told her that she was dangerously off course.

Then I saw *him*, the man who was training her to get about the city independently. Saw him leaning against a lamppost, his arms folded over his chest. Watching, just watching, while she stood there in the middle of the street, in the utter blackness of her affliction, completely disoriented.

By now I was inside the church, observing the scene from a small window in the entrance. I screamed at him silently. "Can't you see she's completely confused? Help her! Have you lost your mind? How would you like to be out there blindfolded?"

Evidently his antennae weren't tilted in my direction, for he made no move. Eventually the girl turned and fumbled her way back to the curb from which she had set out.

She spoke in the direction of the lamppost. But there was no relenting on the man's part, no pity, almost an indifference.

Once more she listened for the movement of traffic as the light turned green for her. Once more she tapped cautiously out into the intersection. This time she angled off to the right, stumbled against the fender of a waiting car, stood for a heartbreaking moment in the middle of the street, then felt her way toward the far curb, hitting it several yards above the intersection. She groped in vain for the sidewalk which wasn't there.

The man (by now I despised him) called something to her across the street. She moved back toward the intersection, found the crosswalk, waited for the light, and moved without a flaw across the street in front of the waiting cars.

Success! I wept and cheered.

Before my astonished eyes the man, that heartless man, came to life. He leaped from the lamppost, bounded toward the girl, and enfolded her in a jubilant bear hug.

So, he had cared after all.

She *had* to stumble, run into things, get lost. She *had* to suffer if she was to be free. And I understood finally that he, hurting for her and a hundred others like her, must be still. He must steel his heart against her need—that she might be free.

There's someone I love, Lord, who's lost and stumbling. He's tried so hard. I've begged You to lead him back to the safe places, but You're leaning on the lamppost, watching. I can't stand it much longer. Is there a reason for Your waiting? Will he, when the struggle is ended, be free at last?

I'm waiting beside You, Lord, trying not to question Your timing. Are You crying too?

Dialogue on Dentists

Recently our family switched dentists. Probably we'd have gone on forever with our old one, except that Don required some nasty root-canal work which required the skills and equipment of a young DDS in town with a shiny new shingle. He came home impressed and as eloquent as he ever waxes (which isn't very) over the "atmosphere."

I giggled. That was a funny word for my man who scorns candlelit restaurants and exotic surroundings. "One needs *atmosphere* for fillings?" I asked, giggling some more.

"Well, there was *something* about the place," he said. Low key, no pressure on the rest of us to change—that's the way he is.

He had to go back several times for what I considered very unpleasant activities, but he didn't complain. In fact, I got the feeling he was quite comfortable about those early-morning appointments.

I was curious but, happily, sound of mouth. However, a few months later, contentedly munching my breakfast granola, I bit down upon something which was neither pecan nor shell, but an ugly hunk of tired filling.

"Where are you going to get it fixed?" Don asked mildly.

"I haven't decided yet," said I, woman-wise.

But you know, don't you, where I headed a few days later? To explore that atmosphere.

The hygienist, in a blue-flowered shirt and navy pants, led me into the torture room, sat me down in a pinkish leather chair, and proceeded to recline me, back, back, until I was horizontal and ridiculously comfortable.

"I'll return," she told me, with a friendly grin.

"I may be asleep," I replied, feeling a bit foolish but pleasantly pampered. Somehow, in that position, my tenseness began to recede and my fears seemed childishly out of place.

When I really did begin to feel sleepy, the flowered shirt returned with a matching companion. This *boy* was going to patch my battle-scarred old molar? this pleasant child in a giddy shirt? Where was the white cardboard coat and the professional air? Atmosphere, indeed!

He inspected my mouth's crooked and patched interior with interest, and reported, "You have good gums. Gums are the real problem, not teeth." Well! Maybe something at the medical school had rubbed off after all.

The female flowered shirt sat down at my head on one side and the degreed flowered shirt on the other. Down from its perch he pulled the familiar tool, and instinctively I tensed. What was the girl there for—to revive me if I fainted? There was a buzzing as whirling metal hit its mark. I waited for the head-jarring vibrations I abhorred, but there were none. The sensation was that of filing a fingernail—painless, not unpleasant. Bonnie, of the blue-green garden, vacuuming from my mouth the water which provided cooling action for the high-speed drill, chatted easily with the matching "garden" across the way, who wielded his various instruments with speed and precision.

"Plenty of tooth left," he affirmed, reassuringly.

His hands, I noted, were warm, comfortable, and competent. It occurred to me that the other doctor's had been cold, efficient, and faintly smelly of antiseptic and nicotine.

Warm hands shouldn't make any difference, but they did. I was absolutely relaxed for the first time ever in a dentist's office. It was comfortable to lie down and to be fussed over by friendly, highly efficient people.

Very hard to define, the difference between past experiences and this. Perhaps Don had said it all in his laconic one word—*atmosphere*. I knew somehow that these two skilled young people were interested in their work, that sparing me all possible pain was their goal— along with keeping my teeth in my head as long as I needed them.

I hate stories that have a moral tacked on the end, but this one wasn't just invented to fit the story. It really did occur to me, driving home that day, that God is like this new dentist: out to make my life, even on our problem planet, as comfortable and happy as possible, if I'd just relax into His expert care. But too often I relate to Him as to a cold professional, ''out to get me''; thus I enter His presence rigid with dread and fear.

Remind me over and over again, Lord, that You too have warm, capable hands.

My Sewing Box Existence

It all started with the sewing box Don gave me for Christmas, a huge three-decker from the Singer Shop with compartments for everything. My fingers itched to transfer the tangle of materials from the tiny, dog-eared box I'd been using for years. Later that day when the Christmas debris had been either organized or ousted, I treated myself to a complete reorganization of my entire sewing area, and very specifically to stocking that fascinating box.

As I sat joyously fitting bobbins into indentations and spools onto spindles, my husband happened by.

"This is absolutely my favorite gift, honey," I said.

I buried my head for a moment on that comfortable shoulder and was suddenly overcome with a foolish urge to cry. "It's so organized," I said in a wobbly voice. "Look at it. There's even a place shaped for scissors. Nothing else in my life has any order anymore, but in that box everything fits."

He laughed at my small storm and assured me I handled our rather chaotic household beautifully. He meant it sincerely, and it was extremely comforting, but my problem still stayed with me.

True, there was nothing orderly about our existence. We had five children, four of them teenagers. During this particular holiday one could find in the front hall a card table topped with the fragile skeleton of a balsa-wood model plane, its builder taking time out from his intricate task only long enough to go snowmobiling now and then. In the family room someone had started a puzzle which must not be disturbed. The living room seemed wall-to-wall bodies as various family members sprawled on the rug with some new game. Don's corner of the family room ran rampant with his medley of hobbies and their related reading material, and lest I leave you thinking that I'm a creature of order trying to survive in this jungle, let me add that my sewing machine was atumble with aqua knit and my desk piled with the clutter of my trade.

It was not all this, however, which had brought on my sense of inner confusion. The house had been full of children and their related activities for a good many years. I am used to it.

I know where it all began. About five years ago I wrote a book. Eventually it was published, and in its wake came a flare of whatever it is that happens to new writers—I hesitate to call it fame. At any rate, it sent me scurrying about the countryside speaking to hundreds of people. New writing opportunities began to arrive in my mailbox. Fan mail, awaiting acknowledgment, lay sorted into piles beside my typewriter. Life was suddenly filled with challenges, and I determined to meet them all. I went about my housekeeping duties with ideas whirling like Frisbees across my mind.

At first it was fun. There was more satisfaction than I like to admit in having written a moderately successful book and gaining a growing recognition as a public speaker. But very gradually I had come to the place where I now found myself. That organized sewing basket really got to me, and I went to my bedroom to face some facts.

I no longer walked in the woods, feeling one with the earth and its Maker.

I no longer baked the bread which our third son loved to smell as he came in from school.

I no longer played games with the children.

Flower gardens, once the joy of summertime, lay frowzy and unkempt.

Worst of all, the daily rendezvous I had always shared with God had become shorter and ever more sporadic. I was too weary to really pray. I could not organize my thinking, even upon my knees.

Of course, in both writing and speaking I had had opportunity to witness for Christ. I did not question that He who gave the talent expected me to use it, but somehow the whole thing had gotten out of hand. Like the old sewing box, my life had become topsy-turvy, tangled, and almost useless.

I realized I faced a crossroad, and that God was trying to tell me something. I had gotten weary enough to listen at last. I'm still praying and searching for His guidance and finding it directly in proportion to how much time I'm willing to spend with Him. Next I want to tell you some of the ways in which He's led, just in case you, too, are caught on some merry-go-round which never seems to stop no matter how vigorously you signal, "Off."

Setting Priorities for Peace

I have talked about my new sewing box and my old life—and how I had asked God to sort things out for me. I *made* time for some extra prayer. As a battle-weary, longtime Christian I knew that had to be the starting point.

For a year and a half I had carried a heavy speaking schedule. Now it began to taper off as I dropped the word here and there that I no longer had time for speaking if I hoped to continue writing. It was a hard thing for me to do, for I love the challenge, the response of listeners. I enjoy people, and writing is often lonely business; speaking is not. Still I also felt a strong sense of relief.

Then a letter arrived from a favorite editor at an extremely busy time. I felt the old familiar knot in my stomach. How could I prepare the article for which he had asked on such short notice? It occurred to me that God had not asked me to sit up into the wee hours of the morning even to exercise the talent which He had given me; so I simply told the editor courteously that I could not fulfill the assignment. It wasn't easy. It will never be easy for me to say No.

Of course, I will go on writing. (I even hope that kindly editor has not crossed me off his list.) But I will not write under pressure. Every truly creative act must find its source in the Great Creator, and how does one hear His whisper when the hour is late, the house untidy, the laundry unsorted, or the children lonely for Mother's companionship? It's taken me a long time to face that question.

Beside my bed, the reading table is piled high with new books just waiting to be read. The pile contains books on nature and religion plus some biographies—all fine reading. I've always managed to squeeze a lot of books into the nooks and crannies of my busy life. But one Sunday as I drove to an early morning lay prayer group, God said to me clearly and unexpectedly, "If you want to get your life untangled, you'll have to read your Bible."

"I *do* read my Bible," I defended. "I've *always* read my Bible."

And He said, "Really?" in that gentle way He has of flashing a light into the murky areas of one's life.

It hit me then that I'd been only fooling myself. I *had been* reading a lot of books *about* the Bible, and I *had been planning* to do some serious study *in* the Bible, but how long had it been since I'd really opened it for anything more than morning worship with the children.

Then He continued, "If you're serious about knowing My will for your life, you'll have to find it in My Word. Put the other books away."

For one wistful moment I thought of all those tempting

volumes, but like a child, long overdue for discipline, I welcomed the counsel. Eagerly I am now setting out upon the new assignment. Where will it lead?

It occurred to me lately that Jesus was certainly a young man with an assignment—a rather sobering one and such a short time in which to fulfill it. Yet as I read the Gospels, I find no sense of urgency. One almost has the feeling He received His daily work assignment from the Father each morning, not worrying about the days or weeks ahead.

He *did* often pray far into the night, which leaves me wondering if prayer is, perhaps, as refreshing as sleep.

We have no evidence He ever worried about impressing anyone or keeping up His image. He maintained a life as orderly, even in its simplicity, as my three-decker sewing box, yet with a thread of purpose glistening consistently through it. Perhaps you and I could live that way if we were to step out beyond our personal ambitions and somehow fit our feet into the tracks of that Young Man from Nazareth.

The Soap Opera Bubble

My young friend Anne called today, and in the course
of our conversation she said, "Our TV goes on when we
get up and goes off when we go to bed. The soap operas
are my friends."

A few hours later the mailman left in our box the
January 12 copy of *Time,* its cover dramatically displaying
two "soap" stars and the legend "Sex and Suffering in the
Afternoon." Because I was still thinking about the morning telephone conversation, I opened to the cover story on
soap operas and read it thoughtfully. It seems my friend is
not alone. Not at all. She is one of more than 20 million
housewives, students, hippies, and the unemployed who
are devoted fans of the soaps.

Anne had said, "With the baby so small I don't get out
much, and I have few friends with whom I feel really
comfortable, anyhow. I have come to think of the people
on the soap operas as my close friends." It startled me a
little when she said that. Could anyone really be so lonely?

Yet *Time* quoted a Duke University student: "It's the
only constant in our lives." A woman, after watching a

25

death on her favorite soap, confessed, "It was not at all like losing a character in fiction of any other kind. I saw the characters in the soaps more often than my friends. . . . It had a continuity stronger even than the news." A doctor requested fewer killings on *Edge of Night* because one of his patients was suffering agonies over the deaths of so many people she felt she knew.

Do we conclude from *Time's* study that a great loneliness has invaded planet Earth, that human beings reach out helplessly to one another for consolation and understanding but do not find that for which they search? Consequently, they sit down before the television and live a pseudolife through the traumas of the soap personalities, until they become not just observers but participants. It *appears* a safe existence. One may weep in empathy over the heroine's problems with a philandering husband, but one's own husband will still come home at night. (He may look a little jaded, however, beside TV's glamour boys—more on that later.)

Somehow I cannot accept such a solution to life. I do not wish to sit on the edge of my seat weeping and biting my nails over the tawdry product of some writer's imagination. There will be tears enough to shed over my own real-life situations, which brings me to another point. It seems we have only a certain quota of emotional reserves for our lifetime. Not one of us will escape having to draw upon them. Between birth and death we will face the loss of those we love, illness, tragedy, and sorrow. But what if we have squandered our allotted share upon the make-believe world of soap opera? or the late movie, for that matter? or the horror shows?

Soap operas also present a telescoped view of life. While we all face moments of great joy and great sadness occasionally, they are usually fairly well spaced. A large percentage of our days are spent in routine activity. Sometimes when we flip off the television, and the beautiful gal with tears glistening on her long (artificial) lashes fades from the screen, we wish we had a lover for whom to weep. We wish someone would say to us in an agony of longing, "My darling, I cannot live another day without you." Instead, friend husband comes in looking just as ordinary as when he left in the morning, demanding crossly, "How come the kids can't get their bicycles off the driveway before I get home at night?"

It's easy to decide at this point that our entire life is a dull mistake. If we look at the normal activities of our days through the distorted glasses of make-believe long enough, we can lose our sense of values completely—even to the point of turning away from all that's meaningful.

Yet just to say that soap operas are a sick way to avoid facing life doesn't solve the problem. We *are* a lonely race, even those of us stacked compactly into cities. In our rushing to and fro we brush against one another in superficial ways, seldom tarrying for any real communion. If soap operas aren't the answer, what is?

In the next chapter I'll share with you something which has been helpful to me, because sometimes I'm lonely too.

Where Are We Running?

And if you and I, each on our own spot of Earth, can find our way out of the shadows and into the sunlight, surely we can lead others there. Then we'll no longer need to anesthetize ourselves with *The Guiding Light* or *As the World Turns*.

Making Life More Exciting

In the previous chapter we talked about the boredom and loneliness which drives humans into the fantasy land of soap operas and related fictional media. We concluded there had to be something better.

If our life is empty and dull, perhaps there is something we can do about it, but we must be willing to turn about and walk into the wind of our habit patterns. It will require change—even if that change for the better sometimes seems frightening. After all, our deadly ruts are safe and familiar.

Perhaps step one would be to leave the television off for the day. (See, I told you change is demanding, but if we're going to trade that pseudolife for *real living*, then we must be willing to attempt new things.)

Now let me suggest a specific way to start the day, preferably before a window in a private place. This may mean rising ahead of the rest of the family, but once you've fought your way out of that cozy bed, it begins to feel like an adventure. Looking out at the dawn, say, "Good morning, Lord. This is the day which You have made. I will rejoice and be glad in it'' (my own paraphrasing of Psalm 118:24).

Then thank Him for five specific things. Not the same five every morning. Use your imagination. Next, make five requests. These may be for yourself, your family, or some friend with a problem. You may want to repeat these requests morning by morning, crossing them off your list as you receive answers or assurance, and adding new ones.

Now, right at the window, before you start your morning activities, pray very reverently, "I invite You, Jesus Christ, into my life, this day, to do with me as You will." Then listen carefully all day for any instructions He may have for you. Keep tuned in. He may have errands that only you can do.

I have asked you specifically to make this early morning contact with your Maker because I believe strongly in the following words of Hubert Van Zeller: "The soul hardly ever realizes it, but whether he is a believer or not, his loneliness is really a homesickness for God." If we can heal this basic loneliness, we will no longer need an artificial environment.

Here are some suggestions for the rest of your day:

Tidy up the house. Do some super-special house-cleaning job which will make you feel very virtuous.

Plan a meal which is nutritiously sound and extra delicious for the dinner hour when all the family will sit down together.

Paraphrase some verses in the Bible—maybe going

through the Book of John at your own pace and putting it in your own words. You'll never be the same again.

Think of something you've always wanted to do and start doing it: taking a course in American literature, making a Bicentennial quilt, painting, taking piano lessons. We have dozens of talents and abilities which lie untapped throughout our lives.

Concentrate on people. Really listen to what *they* are saying. Chat with your youngster when he comes in from school. (If he's always had to share you with "Another World," he'll be overjoyed with your complete attention.)

Do something special for your husband. Even if your marriage has been in the doldrums for ever so long, treat him tonight as if you'd been counting the moments until his arrival. Hug him and say, "Thanks a million for all you do for the kids and me." He really is special, you know. We just commit that ugly act of taking each other for granted day after day until sometimes the marriage withers and dies, but it will usually revive with a bit of attention.

Call a friend or have a neighbor over for lunch; exchange a few words with a stranger at the grocery store or in an elevator. Phone a fellow church member you've never known very well and just get acquainted.

Visit someone who's sick and take along a casserole; baby-sit for a harried young mother; tutor a child who's having school problems.

Enjoy your body and your good health. Include some sort of outdoor activity in your daily program. Take

31

a bicycle ride, play tennis, do exercises, work in the garden, mow the lawn, paint the garage, play hopscotch with the kids, walk with your husband in the evening, climb a mountain, go swimming.

Now, who in the world has time for soap operas??

The World Needs More Compassion

Out of the corner of my eye, I noted the temperature gauge flashing a red warning. Almost at the same instant steam began to spray out from beneath the hood of our Buick station wagon. I pulled off to the side of the road and watched helplessly as the contents of the radiator boiled in a murky stream across the highway.

Fortunately there were four or five houses nearby, so making a phone call shouldn't be difficult. But after knocking patiently, and futilely, at four doors, I wasn't so sure. This must be a neighborhood of working women. Well, there was one more house, and I could hear voices and a radio playing—surely hopeful signs.

I pushed the doorbell, and inside somewhere a chime responded pleasantly. It was a split level, and just above my head a teenager raised a window and yelled impatiently, *"What d'ya want?"* Either she or the chime was in the wrong house.

I explained that my car had broken down, and I needed only to make a phone call.

"Wait a minute. I'll ask my mother."

Where Are We Running?

I admired the long sweep of manicured lawn, the bed of pink geraniums at the doorstep. The day, young and still endowed with dew and possibilities, made it hard to be anything but optimistic on such a morning.

The frowzy teenager returned and pressed her nose against the screen. "Sorry, my mother says we're not up and about yet. You'll have to go to the neighbors."

"There's no one home," I answered meekly. "I tried them all."

"Oh?"—a faint relenting.

From another room a strident voice slashed the August morning. *"Shut that window, Mary. I told you to tell her it's too early. There's nobody downstairs yet."*

My watch said 9:22.

The window closed. I made my way back along the driveway, down the road toward my wounded car, and on some distance in the other direction toward a lone house, where fortunately I met a warmer reception.

Months later I read Terrence Des Pres's study of prisoners of war entitled *The Survivor*. He analyzed, after intensive research, the reasons why some prisoners survived the horrors of German and Russian prison camps while others died. He shares several conclusions, all of them enlightening and sobering.

There was, first of all, the element of what he termed "luck." Those too old, too young, and too ill were soon eliminated. Second, there was among the survivors a universal self-respect, a kind of dignity in the most awful surroundings. These people attempted to maintain a form of cleanliness, when no real cleanliness was possible.

Another characteristic common to all survivors was a fierce will to live which could not be snuffed out by filth, starvation, beatings, and every imaginable suffering. Des Pres says large numbers of men and women died because "they failed to strive for life with every fiber of their being."

But the conclusion which most interested me as a Christian was that *only those individuals who retained their compassion and concern for others came home*. He quoted one Treblinka survivor as saying, "In our group we shared everything; and the moment one of the group ate something without sharing it, we knew it was the beginning of the end for him."

Des Pres shares a quote from the book *Night* by Elie Wiesel. An "old" prisoner is speaking to new arrivals: "We are all brothers, and we are all suffering the same fate. The same smoke floats over all our heads. *Help one another. It is the only way to survive.*"

For some reason my thoughts turned to my friends of the split level on the sunny August morning. I wondered how they would have fared at Auschwitz . . . or how any of us would have for that matter.

I Cared, Ellen, I Really Did

Today my friend died. Not neatly of disease, but willfully, the victim of some awful despair. She was married to a successful man, a man she loved. Two handsome, intelligent teenage sons both challenged and delighted her. At home, at the country club, or on the ski slopes, she was a woman of today: assured, chic, and in control. Or so it seemed.

We talked, not so long ago, in her spacious bedroom. She had been ill but was, she insisted, on the mend. Smoke curled lazily from her ever-present cigarette as we chatted.

I noted dark circles beneath intelligent gray eyes, tension underlying witty conversation. We talked of the ordeal through which she had just passed, discussed a writing project on which she was working, and made mother-talk about our sons.

As I drove home from that visit I wondered why she had asked me to come. I knew we had not touched the real reason. Skirted it, perhaps, but that was all.

And now, with April's bright invitation to live splashed over earth and sky, I must grapple with her death;

for my kitchen phone has jangled its ugly news into my morning.

While I tidy the shelves, my memory is a montage of Ellen—her sleek little cap of dark hair; her quick, lithe movements; her husky speech, its New York accent falling strangely on my small-town ear.

Ellen coming down the front walk in a white tennis outfit, stunning in its simplicity.

Ellen introducing her oldest son, motherly pride escaping her sophistication.

Ellen teaching my youngest to swim with a patience I'd never exercised toward another's child.

Ellen's hurried, indifferent handwriting in my mailbox.

Ellen's voice saying, "Do you have time to stop by? I really need to talk to you."

Suicide has become common, I tell myself, as my hands automatically load the dishwasher. People are uptight today. One never knows who's hurting or how desperately. How does one tell? Freddie Prinze; Sylvia Plath; the boy down the street; Ellen—the famous and the ordinary.

How could I have known?

What could I have done?

Or *did* some secret, subconscious part of my being know—but knowing, tremble to dig beneath the surface, beneath that layer with which we insulate ourselves from others, wanting them to discover our deepest hurts but too proud to let them?

Where Are We Running?

If I had it to do over, I'd say, "Ellen, why did you ask me to come? Tell me the *real* reason. Let's be done with this talk about writing and our sons."

I would pray with her. *I* have no magic healing for despair (sometimes I am almost overcome by my own), but *God* does. I would swallow the foolish pride which said, "One does not suggest prayer to this woman of the world who has it all together."

I would read to her the words from the Scriptures that once literally saved me from mental collapse at a time of stress.

I would call her more often to be sure her world was right side up.

I'd invite her out for lunch, even though my tight schedule rarely allows me the luxury of guests.

Perhaps in the end it wouldn't have made any difference, one person's caring. But I shall never know. The wondering will haunt me all my days.

Gift From Doris

Down upon my knees, I scoured the kitchen floor with Soilax and tears. Our cozy apartment, snug against the winter darkness, held no comfort this night. It wasn't really *ours* anymore, just mine. Uncle Sam had snatched my husband away, putting my patriotism severely to the test.

The hours spent at the office I could manage, but from the moment the home key turned in the lock, those eerie rooms began closing in on me. I had fallen into a dull routine. A cold snack in the name of dinner, a long tender epistle to the source of my loneliness, and then on to household tasks which I had rigidly portioned out among the days of the week.

Upon the stairs I heard much stomping of feet, then a sudden sharp knock at the door. I knew before shouting, "Come in" that it would be friend Doris. She stood in the doorway smiling, restraining an eager wet cocker upon his leash.

"Get up from your knees, girl. It's our kind of night. Let's go for a walk."

Where Are We Running?

We both loved the evenings when snow fell softly and our boots left only noiseless indentations to prove our passing. We were new friends, and our shared pleasure in the still white world was a wonder to both of us. But this was Thursday, floor-scrubbing night, I explained carefully, and after the floors, I would wipe off the woodwork and do the laundry.

From her puddle in the hall, Doris cocked an amused eyebrow. "You'll always have floors to scrub, but there's only one tonight."

Suddenly I saw the dull victim of routine I had become. Only an idiot would have gone on polishing and weeping. Leaving the scrub pail at the halfway point, we shuffled out into the misty world where streetlights beckoned blurredly through falling flakes. I still remember, though many years have passed, the warm, good conversation, the black cocker climbing and falling among the drifts, and the totally alive sensation I had not experienced since my husband's departure. *Indeed, that night would never come again.* Absurd that I had to be told. There are times when we must stick to the task at hand, but it's a wise person who knows there are moments—lovely, fleeting fragments of life—when it doesn't pay to be so splendidly sensible.

Last spring my youngest came banging excitedly through the back door. "Daddy's going to drag some logs down from the woods with the tractor. Come with us."

Piles of sorted clothes awaited my attention in the laundry room. The dinner hour was not far distant, and about me at the desk lay the scattered efforts of my day's work, page after page of book manuscript. The ever-present deadline crouched upon my shoulders.

Outside, May hovered, fragile and fleeting as the first butterfly.

Amy awaited my decision. Eleven years old. Hardly child. Not yet teenager. Sunlight had sifted a dusting of freckles across her nose. There was about her the elegant awkwardness of a young colt, the sun-kissed glow of an earth-child. Long hours at the typewriter had left me like a pale, bent weed unearthed beneath a log.

Leaving my main character with an uncompleted sentence dangling from her mouth, I rose stiffly.

"Are you *really* coming?" she delightedly sparkled.

We fitted ourselves into the tractor's odd corners, and the driver took my hand as we jolted off up the newly plowed hillside. Don heard his first white-throated sparrow of the season, Amy and I found bloodroot blossoming among last year's curling leaves, and the land was a wonder and a healing to us all. Over the years I heard my young friend of long ago saying, "You'll always have floors to scrub, but there's only one tonight." I count that advice one of the best gifts I've ever received.

Please Ride Carefully, Son

We were riding into town to buy a red shag rug for his dormitory room at boarding school—I in the family station wagon, our sixteen-year-old son behind on his Kawasaki 500. As I maneuvered my way in and out of traffic on a busy highway, he flitted along in my wake. Though he'd ridden a field bike for years, his road license was pretty new. I hadn't, in fact, seen him on the highway before. Through my rearview mirror I observed the sure way in which he rode—almost a dance-like rhythm in his movements, he and the machine as one.

I knew that good feeling of leaning on the turns, the perfect pitting of balance against speed. His father and I, in the early years of our marriage, had wandered all over the eastern coast on a big Indian cycle, and my father before me had shocked the New England countryside with his daring along the dusty roads of his home valley. Oh, he came by it honestly enough, this son of mine. I watched him with pleasure, deciding that a skilled cyclist was a thing of beauty, just as is a skilled horseman.

But suddenly all my proud motherly musings were

shadowed by a keen awareness of his vulnerability. 'Twould take but one mistake on his part or that of a fellow traveler to send his young body hurtling across concrete. I remembered the cocky arrogance of my own youth, the assumption that death was for the old. But I also knew this particular boy had witnessed, that very summer, a car accident in which a young woman had been killed. It had been a sobering experience, giving him—I hoped—a new respect for life. Even so, before we entered the home-furnishings store, I delivered a long lecture on the perils of the highway.

Sometimes we must nearly lose life before we appreciate it. On page 110 of his book *The Year of My Rebirth*, American writer and poet Jesse Stuart, resting under giant beech trees while recuperating from a near-fatal heart attack, wrote, "The beech leaves above and around me have made unnecessary the things I thought I had to do. They have destroyed the habits I thought I had to obey. They have taken away the ten pipes a day I thought I would never be able to do without. In their stead they have substituted clean wind for my lungs. These natural pleasures have been so satisfying that I am left to wonder why man is always burning with his ambitions, his desires to accumulate, his great competitiveness, his wild impulse to excel his fellowmen."

Admiral Byrd wrote in his book *Alone* that he learned, in his icebound shack awaiting death, nothing mattered but the relationships with those he loved. All his long pursuit of knowledge and fame seemed as nothing then.

Where Are We Running?

Solomon discovered, after abandoning himself to all the sensual and secular indulgences of his day, that only God mattered.

It's unfortunate that we often have to look death square in the eye or tiptoe far out onto the quicksands of sin before we are able to marshal our priorities. We take the gift of life for granted, hurt those we love, and hurry by the rosebush at the back door, day after day, without ever noticing small tight buds opening to pink perfection.

I once thought that to see my name in print, to be sought out as a speaker, would fulfill my every desire. Wiser now, I know the price is long hours huddled over a typewriter and lonely nights away from home and family. Let me sit instead beside our pond, watching the wind ruffle diamonds across its sunlit surface.

Life is very precious. So ride carefully, my son.

The Twenty-Five-Year Glue

I'm quite useless during September. All I want to do is wander about outside, admiring frowsy mums and late-blooming roses. There's something hypnotic about the sun, which no longer burns, but warms one soothingly all the way through, tart air, meanwhile, reminding you it's not June.

There's a limb on one of our front yard maples that just can't wait. About midmonth it bursts into premature flame, looking a bit silly among its green fellows. I call it my "anniversary bough" and would feel a mite miffed if it failed to appear in full dress on the fourteenth. Last September was a bit special, for Don and I celebrated twenty-five years together on that date. The old tree draped her frivolous limb in a splendid assortment of red-gold bangles almost as if she knew.

We had planned only a routine day of gratitude for the good life God has given us. But as we were about to prepare the evening meal, in trooped a group of friends, bearing a tall, tiered wedding cake and a potluck dinner. As their wishes for our continued happiness rained upon

45

us, I fought off foolish tears and concentrated on the wondering face of our eight-year-old as she grasped the fact that her parents were the objects of this delightful plot. Somehow she had always pictured us on the giving end of surprises. In fact, she wasn't quite sure it was respectable for adults to be involved in such nonsense. Finally, however, she tossed her musings aside, grinned at me shyly, as if we'd never met before, and gave herself over to contemplation of the snow-castle cake.

Later, when the guests had departed, leaving bows and wrappings in the living room to remind us of their love, I fell to pondering the mysteries of marriage. Why are some couples happy, others not? What had Don and I learned about this ancient institution in twenty-five years together? We had achieved a compromise sort of thing that worked for us, probably because we discovered early that it's better to accept each other as is than to attempt a remodeling project. For instance, Don might prefer that I stick to housewifery rather than involving myself in various writing ventures, but he knows I'd be less than a whole person if he asked it of me, so he doesn't. In fact, he takes pride in my small successes.

On the other hand, I do not share his enthusiasm for classical music, or rather the volume at which he plays it, but I seek my own quarters at a distant point in the house and let him pursue his pleasures in peace.

We have learned that many a quarrel may be averted by Solomon's "soft answer" (Proverbs 15:1), and that "I'm sorry" is a healing phrase when the situation does get out of hand. (Don, I hate to admit, says it much more gracefully than I do.)

We don't do a lot of things together, a practice which is supposed to be disastrous. I'm not so sure. We've learned a lot from each other's interests in a painless, osmosis sort of way. The important things we share—love for our children, deep pleasure in country life, a common bent toward thriftiness, an eye for colonial houses, and, most vital, our faith in God. This faith is the glue that cements our differences and glosses our imperfections. When we kneel, hands linked across the bed each night, the problems of the day slink away. They know such praying partners are formidable foes indeed.

It's been a good twenty-five years, Don.

For Better or for Worse

I envy today's brides who are wed in apple orchards and who create their own vows, discarding the formal ceremony, even that controversial word "obey" if they so desire.

If I could turn back the years, I'd be married out-of-doors myself, in early October, with the torch leaves spinning lazily down. I'd wear a long, simple blue cotton dress that matched the sky, and I'd probably write a carefully worded pledge, because writing is my business; but it wouldn't mean a great deal, for until one is put to the test, it's difficult to know just what one has to give.

Once, in the early days of our marriage, Don and I sat at the kitchen table budgeting, as usual, our combined paychecks. We had agreed at the start to give to God our tithe, plus a generous offering each week, pay our bills, and then rush the rest to a savings account before we were tempted to let it slip through our fingers.

We placed the portion for God in a church envelope and sorted the rent, food, and insurance into the compartments of a labeled folder. (There were no installment payments, for we had vowed from the beginning to buy nothing for which we could not pay cash.) The thirty dollars or so left over my young husband shut between the pages of the savings account book in preparation for his weekly trip to the bank.

To his utter bewilderment, the frugal bride of whom he'd been so proud burst into tears. "I hate saving money," she said bitterly. "Save, save, save. That's all you can think of."

"Why, honey, I thought we agreed we wanted a house and that it was worth a bit of sacrifice. I never dreamed you were unhappy. What is it you want?"

The perverse girl cried harder. "I don't know *what* I want, but I never earned any money before, and it's just whisked right out of my hands before I even have time to think about it." Peeking between her fingers, she saw his puzzled face, knew she was being impossible, but she couldn't stop. "Maybe *you* like running around with a dollar bill in your pocket all week, but I'd like to *buy* something for a change."

"Then you just have yourself a spree," he said, handing her the money. Amusement flickered at the corners of his mouth, making him seem old and wise and her more contrary than ever.

"I don't want the wretched stuff. Just tuck it away in that old bank and let it mold."

Then he did exactly the right thing. He sat down and pulled her, stiff and resisting, onto his lap. "I don't blame you a bit, sweetheart. We *have been* living on a pretty tight budget. Let's take the savings this week and do something for fun with it. I never thought about this being the first money you've ever earned.'' (He didn't mention that he'd never indulged in any lush living himself.)

And that silly child of long ago smiled through her tears and said, ''I'll put my half in the bank if you will. You're all the fun I *really* need.''

So perhaps his vows, had he created them himself, might have gone something like this:

''I will love you when you are impossible, try to understand you when you don't make any sense, spoil you when you don't deserve it, and lead you gently toward maturity.''

Hers? What *have* I given him through the years? All the surprises that living with a woman involves? a bit of laughter? my loyalty? I really don't know. You'll have to ask him.

The Marriage Money Maze

"You'll never guess what Vance gave me for my birthday." Gray hair curled softly forward about the pretty, eager face before me. Large china-blue eyes sparkled with delight. What had brought such pleasure to this old friend to whom life had given a successful husband, six handsome children, and every good thing? What unusual bauble had Vance discovered?

"Well, hurry and tell me," I urged. "I haven't seen you glow like this in years."

She opened her purse and produced a pale blue, very feminine checkbook with her name engraved in one corner. "My very own checking account," she said shyly, wondering if I'd laugh. "He put $200 in it and will add to it each month. I may do just as I please with the money."

"And what is this liberated lady planning to do with her wealth?"

"Stop teasing, or I'll not tell you," she cautioned. "For years I've wanted to make an annual contribution to the university which I attended, but our expenses were

51

heavy, with the children in college, and I was afraid Vance would think it an unnecessary expense. That's where my first check went. In fact, I've not spent a penny beyond that. I'm just basking in the idea that I don't have to *ask* anymore."

"Did you ever go without anything important?" I pursued, knowing money had been more plentiful in her home than in most.

"No, of course not," she answered thoughtfully. "I knew I was free to shop for the family's needs without question, and that even luxuries were available to me, but often I felt some unexplainable guilt if I spent money on books, clothes, or frivolous things for myself, even though Vance urged me to do so. Somehow, not having to explain where this money goes is the most delicious freedom ever."

"Are you going to save up for a mink stole or a trip to the Caribbean?" I asked, wondering what secret whims she entertained.

"No, but I *am* going to enroll my cleaning lady in a book club she's been yearning to join. She's struggling single-handed with her son's education and has to skip all the extras for a few years."

"Now that's what I call extravagance!" I laughed gently at this delightful woman. We went on to discuss the female position in the marriage money maze. In a good union the husband usually wants his wife to have all the necessities and as many luxuries as he can afford, but how he offers it makes all the difference in the world.

The Marriage Money Maze

If he says, "What's mine's yours, honey. Just tell me what you need," there enters in a disturbing factor. It's as if he says, "Submit a request, and if it's reasonable, I'll be glad to oblige."

Women put in long hours, often much longer than men, at tasks husbands would be hard put to handle if their mates were suddenly to disappear. Who else knows Johnny can't do math in the evening because he's too weary? that Kathy will have a cold all winter if she skips her vitamin C? that Bill will eat only peanut-butter sandwiches in his lunch and that Nancy is allergic to bananas?

It's an old story that a wife and mother juggles a dozen roles throughout the day, yet manages to seem at leisure and available to whoever may need her attentions. She shouldn't feel guilty when buying a bunch of violets for the coffee table or a new blue sweater that matches her eyes, but she often does.

It's the gift bestowed with no strings attached which allows a woman the financial dignity she deserves. (After all, what man must ask for his paycheck each week, reminding his employer he has mouths to feed, car payments to meet, and enjoys an occasional round of golf?)

My own Don laid a fifty-dollar bill on my dresser the other day. As he had already given me my monthly allotment for household expenses, I asked the obvious: "What's that for?"

"For whatever silly thing you might be too polite to request," he replied, tongue in cheek, for though I might not ask for a specific item, I've been known to hint quite broadly that my personal purse was pretty flat.

If you're still stuck in the asking routine, leave this book open on his reading stand. Perhaps he'll take the hint. His response may be a little or a lot, depending upon his income or his generosity, but be it five or fifty dollars, it spells dignity and allows one to wash the dishes without self-pity.

I Wouldn't Trade Places With Any Man!

If you were to ask twenty housewives how they felt about being women, you'd probably get twenty different answers, for we're all a bit confused concerning our role these days. It used to be enough if our children were mannerly and we knew what to do with herbs, but today those accomplishments, in some gatherings, would be considered a mite backward.

So, we begin to *think,* a new activity for some of us women, and try to evaluate what there is to be had from the role in which fate has cast us. First of all, do we *like* being women? Or are we angry that we weren't the firstborn son? We could get out our college psychology books and toss that one around for awhile, or line up a good counselor and try to talk our frustrations away, but it's a lot simpler (and cheaper) just to say, "Well, here I am, walking Planet Earth with my gender all decided," and take it from there. Happiness is usually more a matter of attitude than of gender. If you are really convinced that men have some advantage, then accept the conviction as a challenge. Not to elbow them in their world, but to find the best of your own. Me, I like being a woman for lots of reasons.

First of all, in most cases, we are closer to people than men are. Because we are sensitive, we know when people hurt and when they rejoice. We understand our children as fathers seldom do.

Second, women are more creative than men. Yes, I know most of the greats have been male—artists, musicians, writers, even chefs. But that's because men are programmed to achieve. Women have been programmed to tend the house and have babies. That kind of setup isn't very conducive to creating symphonies and pursuing Pulitzer prizes. A few have managed such successes, however. The rest have played their assigned role, not unhappily, and have managed to *create* every day of their lives in unspectacular ways.

She looks, this woman of the home, upon her tawny-eyed son and knows when she shops for a sweater or sports coat for him that brown is his color.

She finds a copper teapot in a secondhand shop and sees it full of blue bachelor's buttons on the coffee table in her Early American living room.

She sets a Bible verse to music and teaches it to her preschooler. And another and another. Years later they are still with him, because he remembers her silvery voice and loving attention as they sang together.

In his book, *Creative Power,* Alex Osborne says, "In all the aptitudes so far found measurable, Jane is just as bright as Joe. Even more so, according to the Johnson O'Connor Foundation, which found from 702 tests of women that their average *creative* talent is definitely higher than the average man's. Based on these tests, the female is as much as 25 percent ahead of the male in relative creativity.''

Finally, we are more tuned-in to beauty. Perhaps that's a cultural thing. Men become immersed in the world of business, in routine, in the clamber toward success, and the beautiful seems irrelevant to their goals. When a woman hangs out the family laundry, she takes time to talk with the swallows teetering companionably upon her clothesline. When she gives the baby its morning bottle, she observes dark lashes feathered against creamy skin, the kissable curve of the cheek. When she kneads bread, she sees the beauty of her own capable, tanned hands as they work the dough into a satiny sphere.

There is in woman a delightful response to color, sound, texture, and form. I would not want to have missed this for the dubious joys of having been general manager of the local department store, or of General Motors, for that matter.

It is not enough, however, to be convinced of our assets. We must put them to some good use. We have no right to clutter the earth, with our femininity as our only excuse for being. Next, we'll discuss what to do with our high privilege of womanhood.

The Privilege of Womanhood

We've talked about the advantages of being a woman. I suppose there are some disadvantages, but you'll have to discuss them with one of the "lib" gals. I've never had time to ponder them. I promised we'd talk about our responsibilities as women, or maybe *privileges* is a better word. I must have been mad to attempt such a weighty topic in the brief space I'm here allotted, but perhaps we can toss a few ideas about, and you can take it from there. (*Remember,* we're highly imaginative beings!)

I used to have a lot of fancy theories about the role of a woman, but at this time in my life it has all sort of spiraled down to a focal point. In the past I often found it difficult to keep my behavior at the level of the standards I had set. I saw a woman as a gentle, creative, strong (yes, it's possible to be both gentle and strong), radiant being. Too often I found myself less than radiant, even somewhat irritable at the edges. Slowly, I have learned that one cannot be all that God had in mind, without God. (That sentence doesn't have the proper rhythm, a technicality with which writers are concerned, but it says all we need to know, so I shall let it stand. In fact, I'd go so far as to suggest that you read it over two or three times.)

The starting point for every woman (be she fifteen or fifty) is the day she says, "God, here I am, delighted with the gift of life, curious to know Your plan for me, and eager to be everything You meant a woman to be. Where do we start?"

You and I are filled with tightly curled buds of possibility, and if the above prayer becomes our daily search, we'll find them blossoming slowly throughout life like some rare, rewarding perennial. You know why I'm so sure of this? Because, since I've used that prayer, and eliminated some of my own frantic scrambling, God has let me do some of the happiest, most unexpected things. I wish I had space to share them with you.

A woman's life seems divided into several stages. First, the preparatory years, and, oh, if we were only wise enough to pray the above prayer at that point! What wonders God could work with a life at its beginnings! How many tears and wrong turns He could spare us! Unfortunately, at seventeen or eighteen a girl usually has little sense of need. Her body is strong, her mind alert, and her confidence almost too healthy. So, often, she must journey down a few dead-end streets before she learns to look upward toward her Maker for direction.

Would it be unforgivably old-fashioned of me to say to any young reader of this column, "Never say 'Yes' to your young man, no matter how promising he appears, until you've taken the matter to God and received His assurance''? All one's future hangs on the right decision at this point, yet how blithely we say the little three-letter word, wedding plans already zinging about in our heads and the strains of "I Love You Truly" teasing our ears. But once the streamers are off the car, it's a long, long journey.

Then comes the era of motherhood—or career if one opts for a childless state—a perfectly acceptable alternative in our day and age, I might add. If you choose motherhood, however (or if perchance it chooses you), by all means do it with flair. Don't stand at the window with big sad eyes watching the mod office girls trip by while your little ones scrap and spill milk. You'd be surprised at how many of those career girls would trade places with you, but even if that were not true, your job is more challenging, more fun, and more creative. Those crazy little kids of yours will be adults someday, and just what kind of adults depends largely on you. Will they have learned from you to

> speak softly,
>
> be kind,
>
> obey God,
>
> respect their father,
>
> plant flowers,
>
> enjoy poetry,
>
> read widely,
>
> appreciate beauty,
>
> exercise their talents?

Or will they grow up helter-skelter, nurtured by television and comforted with cola while their mother drinks coffee with a neighbor and grumbles about the second-rate role of housewife? The role of woman was meant to be beautiful, but it *can be* ugly.

Once the children are pretty much on their own (don't be impatient if it seems to take a long time; nothing else you ever do will be as important), it's time to set out upon your own interests, providing your husband doesn't object—and if you consulted God at the beginning, I don't think he will. Give him and your home plenty of attention, but there will be time left over. Again one is faced with a choice. She may sit down and become neurotic or use prayer, which at this point in life, hopefully has become a habit. You'll find that God is full of plans for you. He will take your creative abilities and use them in constructive and joyful ways. He will take your tenderness and bandage the hurts of His suffering ones. He will take your understanding and minister to His troubled ones. He will take your laughter to His depressed. And the more He spends you, the richer you'll become.

A woman should be daffodils and sunshine, gentleness and Beethoven's Fifth. Band-Aids and kisses.

Bloom Where You Are Planted

Though it is now rather common poster material, I first saw the chapter title some years ago in the home of my friend Connie. She had created a felt wall hanging, bright with flowers, among which the words *Bloom Where You Are Planted* tumbled about. I carried the new thought in my mind a long time. Perhaps because I'm often fantasizing about what might have been—*if* I'd acquired more education, *if* I'd not married so young, *if* I'd not squandered the golden years, *if* I were smarter, *if* I were more talented.

The fact is, however, that right now I'm very much *planted* here at Elm Valley Farm as the mother of five teenagers and wife of a man who prefers his mate in the kitchen doing housewifely things (though he allows her, with good grace, the freedom to pursue those activities relating to her minicareer as a writer).

Even at the age of forty-nine I keep muttering about going back to college. (The local one perches tantalizingly on a hilltop just down the road.) But somewhere deep inside I know it will never be. There are too many rooms in this old house clamoring to be cleaned, too many jeans to be washed, too many writing and speaking commitments to fill.

Let's face it. I'm never going to make *Time's* best-seller list. I'll never do noble deeds for underprivileged people on some foreign soil. I'll never be a psychiatrist, or even a social worker. No one is going to "transplant" me into yesterday's dreams. It's quite possible God never wanted me doing those things anyway. Maybe I was meant to be a petunia by the back door instead of a scarlet rambler on the garden gate.

After that moment in Connie's kitchen, I began to ponder the possibilities of blooming in my own nondescript nook. It occurred to me that in all my scramblings to transplant myself to some more exotic soil, I'd neglected my surroundings. The house was drab, sorely in need of redecorating. I dreaded the decisions, the removal of hundreds of books, long sessions with a paintbrush—but today the living room is fresh and new, blue-green wallpaper contrasting crisply with white woodwork and ruffled curtains. The window in the book-wall is filled with plants, and the floor around the braided rug is waxed and shining.

Deciding our meal planning had become repetitious, daughter Lori and I began adventuring through stacks of recipes which we had clipped from magazines and hoarded over the years.

A new work schedule and weekly menu plan freed me to pursue a college level required reading list. Probably as close to college as I'll ever get, but already it's opened new areas of thought. More time for Bible study too. There's no greater mind expander than an attempt to think the thoughts of God after Him. More valuable than all the classics of man combined, I would guess.

The other day I stumbled upon two paragraphs from that marvelous little book *Happiness Homemade* which should challenge every housebound woman to bloom— joyfully—right where she's planted.

"God assigned woman her mission: and if she, in her humble way, yet to the best of her ability, makes a heaven of her home, faithfully and lovingly performing her duties to her husband and children, continually seeking to let a holy light shine from her useful, pure, and virtuous life to brighten all around her, she is doing the work left her of the Master, and will hear from His divine lips the words, 'Well done, good and faithful servant, enter thou into the joy of thy Lord.'

"These women who are doing with ready willingness what their hands find to do, with cheerfulness of spirit aiding their husbands to bear their burdens, and training their children for God, are missionaries in the highest sense."

A Word for Wives

A young woman penned me some enthusiastic lines, saying she had been hovering indecisively between career and mother roles, but that my article on the rewards of motherhood had renewed her conviction that her first responsibility was to home and children. She was even challenged to approach her homemaking tasks with joy and creativity.

That was a year ago. Yesterday I received another letter from the same young woman. She is now teaching, taking graduate courses, and running her home as best she can among these other activities. I chuckled. She had sincerely desired to become 100 percent homemaker, yet another part of her longed to be out there contributing in the "real" world. Because the same contradictions war within me, I had no criticism for her life-style. I am searching, as is she, for answers. Not only to the motherhood-career role but to the wife-husband relationship.

I have read so many books lately on woman's role that my head is swimming. The liberationists advocate that I stomp my feet and demand my rights, while many Christian writers solemnly refer me to Ephesians 5:22-24. In case you are not familiar with those verses and don't feel like looking them up, here they are:

"Wives, *submit yourselves unto your own husbands,* as unto the Lord. *For the husband is the head of the wife,* even as Christ is the head of the church: and he is the saviour of the body. Therefore as the church is subject unto Christ, *so let the wives be to their own husbands* in every thing."

However much I may prefer the liberated stand, as a follower of Jesus Christ, I must give full consideration to the above words.

I am by nature a person of strong opinions and will hereby confess that the word *submit* falls with discord upon my reluctant ear. I have some questions:

Must the Christian woman bow to her husband's superior (?) wisdom in every area? Wouldn't this eliminate all lively debate?

Suppose the husband were wrong, even morally wrong, in his decision? Must one back him even then? After all, husbands are just ordinary humans with stubborn problem areas of their own.

Must I, as a Christian in an age when women are basking in various new freedoms, learn a new discipline of submission?

As I reread these questions I denote a negative ring to each one. This warns me that I must give sober thought to my own attitudes. Is it possible, if I begrudge my husband his position of power in the family, that I also bow with reluctance before divine authority? I have long understood that our salvation hangs upon this issue of submission to God, upon our awareness that we are only *creatures*, subject ever to Him who conceived the intricacies of our being in His unsearchable mind. Perhaps I need to explore greater depths of submission. I pray a new prayer. *"Lord, teach me true submission to You and to Don."*

As I understand it, the Biblical order for the family goes like this: Christ is at the head; next in the chain of command comes the husband and father, subject to Christ; then the wife and mother, subject to both Christ and husband; last the children, subject to all three. Though I have not always lived by this code, it occurs to me that it would be a great relief to place the responsibility for all final decisions in my husband's lap. There would be a new kind of freedom in letting him bear the anxieties and concerns of our large and complex family. (Just thinking about it sends me into a tailspin of sympathy for him. It sounds like a lonely and difficult assignment.)

But on the other hand, I was made to be his helpmate (Genesis 2:18); so doesn't that give me liberty to make intelligent suggestions, to pray with and for him as he exercises his role of leadership? Of course! But I must also be willing to accept his final decision—whether or not he utilized my suggestions—without sulking, holding a grudge, or even worrying about the outcome. That's a new discipline for me.

Surely God knew when He set the husband in a position of command that errors would be made. Do you suppose God will, if both husband and wife seek faithfully to fulfill their roles, compensate for these errors, or will He, by divine guidance, steer the praying father away from wrong decisions?

In our next chapter we shall discuss other aspects of this matter. I shall even have a word for husbands. In the meantime experiment with some of the ideas expressed above and see how it works out in your marriage.

Love, Honor, and Obey?

We have described a marriage structure which places Christ at the head of the home, the husband next in command, then the wife, and finally the children. This arrangement, however, requires *submission*—to God, to mate, and to parent. It would not appear to be a very popular experiment in this age of liberation. I would not even attempt to sell you on the idea if it were not Biblical, but how can we argue with the Originator of the plan?

But, you say, suppose my husband is not a follower of Jesus Christ and his decisions regarding the children are not in accordance with my Christian principles? Peter has the answer for this, and a very clear and simple answer it is, leaving no room for uncertainty.

"Likewise you wives, be *submissive* to your husbands, so that some, though they do not obey the word, may be won without a word by the behavior of their wives, when they see your reverent and chaste behavior" (1 Peter 3:1, 2, RSV).

Often it seems women respond more naturally to the gospel than do men. Unfortunately we then sometimes

69

assume a spiritual haughtiness which robs our mates of their rightful position as head of the house. This attitude on our part has a tendency to bring out the worst in husbands, causing them to become stubbornly indifferent to God. I am fascinated by the picture Peter paints of the respectful, godly wife who walks serenely beside her unbelieving husband, but I am well aware it's a tough assignment, requiring much prayer. It's hard enough to be submissive to the husband whose goals match one's own.

I would recommend for your reading in this area *The Feminine Principle* by Judith Miles; also Larry Christenson's marvelous book *The Christian Family*. Both books are available in most Christian bookstores.

Then I would suggest that you and I put these principles into practice. For starters, let's try to anticipate our husbands' needs and wishes. Let us not criticize or belittle them in any way. Let's abide by their decisions, even though they may seem all wrong to us. (Remember I told you in the last chapter that it's the helpmate's privilege to make suggestions and to pray with her partner during times of stress in the home but not to insist upon having her own way.)

Laura was a highly intelligent, talented, and spiritual woman. Every prospect upon which she focused her attention seemed to prosper. She helped both her church and community. She loved her Lord fervently, and that love spilled over onto everyone . . . or almost everyone. Her husband, Bill, was a silent man, tart tongued upon those occasions when he chose to speak. But it seemed he

scorned Laura's church most of all. I often marveled that this splendid woman had attached herself to such a drab mate.

Once in our conversation she hinted that she somehow felt sex had little part in a Christ-filled life. The physical aspects of marriage seemed too evil for her participation. I looked at her husband a little differently after that.

A few years later Bill began attending church. At times he seemed almost jovial. His attitudes became more tolerant, and in time he was baptized. One day I said to Laura, "What ever happened to Bill? He's a new person."

She smiled ruefully. "The Lord made plain to me that I had no right to deny Bill a normal marriage relationship. It was a very difficult assignment for me, but slowly I began to show him affection, just touching him, making physical contact, letting him know I was willing to submit, not only to his authority but to his lovemaking." She hesitated shyly. "We are very happy," she declared. "I cheated us both so many years."

So if we have been too "righteous" to meet our husbands' physical needs, perhaps we need to learn submission in that area too. Good luck! I'll be thinking of you as I practice my "yes sirs!"

Shortcuts to Richer Living

Over and over among women I hear the same complaint. "I could accomplish so much if I could only get organized. The days just seem to slip through my fingers." These are women who wish to do something beyond their housework, and I believe every woman worth the label longs to contribute more than her cooking-cleaning talents to the world.

Do not misunderstand me. I'm all for tidy houses, clean, well-cared-for children, and balanced meals, but some of us are convinced there should be a couple of extra hours or more during the day after these activities are completed—depending, of course, in which stage of the child-raising stint one is involved. (Preschoolers are usually a challenging, full-time job.)

I, myself, am often frustrated with the need to fulfill a writing assignment, prepare for a speaking engagement, study for a teaching situation, only to be confronted with the endless tasks of keeping a household clean, happy, and well fed. So I have begun to look around—to listen—and to ask questions. How does the achieving woman manage? What are her secrets? Here are a few of the hints I came up with.

When reading a new magazine, have a pair of scissors at hand to clip all desired coupons, recipes, poetry, articles, housekeeping hints. This eliminates going through the magazine a second time later.

Keep things simple in the home. Avoid useless knick-knacks requiring endless dusting.

Avail yourself of timesaving appliances as the budget allows.

When building or remodeling, plan easy-care surfaces.

A young mother, building a minicareer in radio during most of the hours in which her children are in school, told me she has two hours between the time she leaves the studio and dinner preparations. During those hours she "works like a fiend," as she put it. First she vacuums through the downstairs and straightens the rooms, then tackles one major cleaning job, such as defrosting the refrigerator, changing all the beds, or cleaning kitchen cupboards. With the help of a Thursday cleaning woman she maintains a spotless home and presents to the world a sort of superwoman image. "The whole secret lies in not wasting a second of that two-hour period," she advised. "Often when I walk through the door, I'm tempted to relax with a hot drink and the day's mail, but I then remind myself that if I wish to lead this career-housewife type of life, I must be willing to work a bit harder than a stay-at-home."

One of the most obvious, but often least-practiced,

solutions to the problem of time in a woman's many-faceted life is to train the children early to share the household burdens. Our own six children all understand that during the summer months they are not free to go about their own activities until the dishes are done, the house tidied, the lawns mowed. Rather than a hardship, it has been, I believe, an asset. The boys, as well as the girls, are well able to care for their clothes, prepare meals, and keep their surroundings clean. Of course, during the school year much less is expected of them, for they too lead busy lives then.

Every woman who wishes to spend part of her day in some creative activity not related to the mother-housewife role must become an efficiency expert. She must put her home first. But when that requirement is met, she is free to discover what contribution is hers to make to the world beyond her home.

So what's for you? A return to college? part-time teaching? work with the elderly or the underprivileged? a ceramics class? a Bible-study group?

Me? I'm writing a book—after the dusting, that is!

Medley of Mothers

One of the sharpest and most painful memories of my childhood centers upon a May afternoon in the small, two-room schoolhouse I attended as a child. The teacher had passed out materials for creating Mother's Day cards: pastel construction paper, small pictures of flowers clipped from seed catalogs, lace paper doilies. My fingers could hardly wait for the assembling.

"Make them as pretty as you know how, children," the teacher said as she helped the tiny ones glue and snip. "Inside the card each of you will write a loving message for your mother."

My enthusiasm died. What had I been thinking of? A message for my mother, indeed! I had no mother. What was I to do with this pile of "pretties" before me? I must do *something*, for it would look very odd to just sit. On the other hand, all the children knew I lived with my grandmother, so they'd surely laugh if I made a card. And the teacher—what would she think if her normally eager-beaver second grader sat back like a dunce?

So simple the solution to make one for Grandma

instead, but no such alternate plan entered my seven-year-old mind. For the first time my heart cried out in a kind of desperate frustration at the mother who lay dead in the village cemetery not far distant. "Why did you leave me? I'm funny and odd without you, and *mother* is just a word I'm not allowed to use."

As unobtrusively as possible I put together some sort of card but printed no word upon it. Fortunately, the teacher, busy with last-minute aid for the all-thumbs group, didn't make her intended tour of inspection. On the way home I threw the card into a brook and watched it sail under the bridge and wrap itself soggily around a rock. Some kind of chest-aching sobs, which I little understood, tore out of me as I wandered along the narrow, dusty road toward home.

But though I was not emotionally mature enough to make a substitute card which said, "I love you, Grandma," I did cherish the plump, gray-haired woman who shaped my life. She gave me of herself as unstintingly as any mother could have. And she had so much to give. A good mind, strong principles, a tender heart, and a singing delight in every new morning. One never shrank from living with Grandma around. When a thunderstorm cracked and rolled among our enclosing mountains, she'd urge me to join her upon the porch and watch the fireworks. A summer rain was wasted if I didn't don bathing suit and dance around among the droplets. "That warm rain looks mighty pretty, and it'll feel even better," she'd say.

When she died in my sixteenth year, I truly lost my second mother.

Three years later I married and acquired Mother No. Three. By some heartwarming coincidence, her name was Alice, the same as Mother No. One's. She has been my loyal friend for twenty-six years. From her I learned many of the niceties of homemaking. She has spelled me through long nights with fussy newborns, done our family mending, loved our children through bad times and good, and refrained from even the tiniest criticism of our disciplinary methods.

We have shared, besides her son, recipes, problems, books, and ideas. Other friends have come and gone, but Toota, as we affectionately call her, is always there.

I have learned from my three mothers the following:

(1) No one who has lost, for any reason, the mother of his birth ever outgrows the secret wanting of her.

(2) A good mother substitute can almost fill the gap, and she can make life richly rewarding.

(3) The badly maligned word *mother-in-law* can hold a wealth of tenderness.

Because at this point in life I am mother, mother substitute, and mother-in-law, I begin to get the total picture of woman's role as the generations come and go. I'm trying to place my feet squarely in the footsteps of those women who've led me with unselfish, eager hands through the twisted corridors of life.

Can Emotions Affect Your Baby?

"I want my child to have a perfect start," she said, this beautiful young woman seated beside me at a banquet. She was tanned, dark haired, and very pregnant.

"How do you propose to do this?" I asked.

Her answer came shyly. She hardly knew me, but enthusiasm for her subject overcame her timidity. "I pray every morning that God will help me to be patient and kind that day, to exercise no angry emotions."

"Well, that's a rare philosophy in today's world," I responded, thinking that the simple white gown she wore was very appropriate. "It's not uncommon to watch one's *diet* carefully during pregnancy, but why are you concerned about your emotions?"

"Oh, I'm very careful about my diet, too, but I have been reading *Happiness Homemade*." She raised questioning eyes. Was I familiar with it?

I nodded.

"You know then that the author has interesting counsel about prenatal influence?"

"Yes, I know, but you are the first woman I've met

78

who's taken it so seriously.''

"It makes sense to me." The girl's dark eyes were sober. "Surely when one loses control of his emotions, either in fear or in anger, it must have an effect upon the unborn child.''

"What does your husband think of all this?''

"He understands the importance of peace in the home, especially now, and treats me like a queen. When some difference arises between us, he just grins and says, 'I concede, for little Joe's sake,' and we both laugh. It has made us very aware of all the foolish arguments we used to have but can do quite nicely without. . . . You've raised a lot of children,'' she spoke carefully in deference to the generation gap yawning between us. "Did you practice these teachings during your pregnancies?''

I chuckled. "Four of our six were adopted, so I didn't have much to say about the prenatal influence in their lives. I wish I could tell you that the two to whom I gave birth were given every advantage in this respect, but the truth is that the circumstances of my life were such during one pregnancy that I was depressed, discouraged, and often reduced to tears of utter despair. I attempted to control my emotions during those stormy months but fear I often failed. The other child was born during a period of serenity, and it didn't require much effort on my part to be a gentle soul.''

"I guess one cannot help the outward circumstances. I've known only happiness,'' she said.

"It's true an expectant mother cannot always control

her environment," I agreed, "but I know now I could have controlled my reaction to negative circumstances by committing my life completely to Christ and letting Him do the worrying."

Suddenly, looking at her sitting there so sincere and young, so concerned about the welfare of her child, I realized how unique she really was. It occurred to me that if God were looking today for a woman to bear a special child, such as John the Baptist, Jeremiah, or even Jesus, that this young woman might just meet the requirements.

Later that night, in the lamplight of our living room, I opened *Happiness Homemade* and reread from page 89, "If before the birth of her child, she [the mother] is self-indulgent, if she is selfish, impatient, and exacting, these traits will be reflected in the disposition of the child. Thus many children have received as a birthright almost unconquerable tendencies to evil.

"But if the mother unswervingly adheres to right principles, if she is temperate and self-denying, if she is kind, gentle, and unselfish, she may give her child these same precious traits of character."

I closed the volume, contemplating lost opportunities, and slipped the bookmark of regret between its pages.

When Parents Act Like Babies

The tiny tousled girl rubbed her eyes wearily as her mother settled into the seat beside me. It was an evening church service, and the guest speaker's fame had traveled before him. The auditorium was packed.

"I wouldn't have missed this for the world," my seatmate whispered eagerly.

I nodded my agreement but wondered about the restless little creature draped sleepily over her shoulder. I felt sure she belonged in her crib at home. The child, hardly more than a babe, was just nodding off when the opening hymn was announced, and as mass singing swelled about her, she began to whimper and squirm. By the time the speaker launched into his opening remarks, the whimpering had turned to sobs. The young mother patted, soothed, and whispered endearment—for the first five minutes— then yanked a bottle impatiently from the case at her feet.

Our seatmates stirred in annoyance, those ahead turning to view the cause of such disturbance. Embarrassed now, the woman yanked the child angrily into a sitting position, hissing threats into the wee ear. "You hush up, or I'm going to spank you hard. Stop that racket!''

The little one cried harder, reaching out for her mother's shoulder in vain. In a frenzy of frustration, the woman shook the child until the curly head bobbed back and forth frighteningly. My heart broke for the toddler. When her mother finally stomped up the aisle in defeat, I feared for the helpless little victim of such wrath.

I see this situation repeated over and over again—in restaurants, grocery stores, airports, gatherings of all kinds. Weary little ones clutching Mother's pantleg or skirt, weeping. Mother irate and loud in her frustration.

''You just straighten up and stop that nonsense.''

''When I get you home, you're going to get it.''

''Do you want a spanking right here?''

Invariably the child cries harder.

Child psychologist Eda LeShan defines the situation well in an article for *Woman's Day* (August, 1975): ''Under the age of five or six there is a kind of exhaustion that comes close to madness. The child feels a deep and total fatigue that destroys his limited ability to make sense out of the external world. It is a feeling of total disorder and confusion. Reality becomes distorted, and the child's whole being is enveloped in helplessness and terror. All he can do is cry like the infant he feels he's become again. But when adults behave as if the child is just being ornery, total panic ensues. There he is, lost in a terrible anxiety in which he knows he's losing control in every aspect of his being, while grown-ups—his only hope of survival—are screaming at him to stop this nonsense and behave.

When Parents Act Like Babies

"The child wants desperately to stop crying. Those adults are his lifeline: to displease them is what he dreads most in the world—and yet he cannot stop. He feels totally out of control, like a plane spinning toward a monstrous crash landing."

Mrs. LeShan suggests finding a quiet spot and assuring the child that you know how dreadful he feels and that you've even felt the same way yourself. Give him the comfort of your arms and your serenity. This is an excellent suggestion—one that requires *maturity* on the mother's part—but it cannot always be arranged in every circumstance. Perhaps another solution would be to avoid situations where the child might become overtired. This requires *sacrifice* on the mother's part, a willingness to forgo some pleasures during the child's early years. For instance, the young mother in my little story would have gained much more from reading her Bible quietly within her home while her pretty girl-child slept peacefully.

And if you do one day find yourself in one of those impossible situations where you are toting suitcases in both hands and a sobbing youngster is climbing your skirt, remember Mrs. LeShan's advice. Sit down on the suitcases, take him on your lap, and whisper, "I know how tired you are. I'm tired too. Let's rest a minute together."

There may be some helpful soul nearby who'll mutter, "What he really needs is a good whack on the bottom."

Don't so much as lift your head. For the sweeter relationship you'll have with your child, you can afford to ignore her.

Gifts Our Children Loved

After sixteen years of doing too much haphazard shopping in the toy department at the holiday season, I've come up with a few conclusions concerning gifts for children. There are only a few worth the money, but those few are every child's right. We have an attic full of errors—games too complicated or too dull, gadgets guaranteed to hold the attention at least ten minutes, toys broken within the first week, and whole shelves of costly items which refused to capture the child's imagination as it has the adult's.

With our children, tricycles, bicycles, and self-propelled tractors or cars were never neglected until they collapsed in rusty relief upon the junk pile. So, although they are expensive toys, they evidently fill some need to emulate the speeding adult population, and they give the child terrific leg muscles in the process. I would say the wheeled vehicles are a must.

For the toddler, one noisy push toy is essential (ours loved the corn-popper model put out by Fisher Price); also, a large set of the best building blocks. These will be used from age two, almost indefinitely. I still like them. There are terrific creative possibilities in all the variety of shape, size, and color. Then, of course, there must be plenty of small cars and trucks to push in and out the bridges and tunnels. Girls enjoy this activity, too, but it helps to have a brother to make the motor noises.

Fisher Price also makes a sturdy wooden train, the cars brightly painted and locking together easily. It follows the child with a delightful clacking noise. We had a double set for the children, and they loved loading the little boxcars, with their sliding doors. A cargo of nuts and raisins right after lunch was their favorite freight.

Later on, Lego blocks became an enduring family favorite. We added to them through the years and constructed unbelievable empires with the gay red and white bricks. These can be enjoyed from age four almost indefinitely and are absolutely indestructible.

Dolls—I'm afraid I've never had a daughter who really liked them, more than momentarily. I've sewed many doll wardrobes at great expense of time, and I feel, for our family at least, it was a waste; the child's pleasure was so fleeting. Surely every little girl should have a doll, and truly maternal little maids should have several, but often it's the *mother* who loves buying all the latest wetting-weeping creations, rather than the child who loves playing with them.

Little girls do love very simple needlework which doesn't drag on too long and muffin and cake mixes. I buy the regular-size mixes to be baked in the family oven.

They seem more practical than the doll-size ones which are gulped down in one bite by heckling brothers.

It's a rare boy who doesn't enjoy building model cars, planes, or ships, but there is always the temptation to buy something beyond the child's capabilities. Unless one is prepared to sit down with the boy and help, better to purchase something he can handle on his own. It's damaging for him to become frustrated, admit defeat, and cast the whole project aside.

An inexpensive and fun gift for a boy or girl is a novelty nutcracker (Sears usually has a few clever ones in its Christmas catalog) and a big sack of nuts.

I've often packed a small, gaily flowered vanity case for a little girl with barrettes, a comb, clear nail polish, bubble bath, perfume, a few bits of change, and a tiny mirror.

At other times it has been a small case filled with Scotch tape, marking pens, writing pads, gummed stars, letters, crayons, bright pictures clipped from magazines, and glue. This is an especially delightful gift for a child who will be traveling a long distance.

At thirteen or fourteen an alert youngster finds a subscription to *Reader's Digest* or *Time* a flattering gift. Because you have assumed he's ready for adult reading, he'll dive in and find to his surprise there's nothing difficult about either magazine. Thus you have opened new doors for him.

How about promising an older child one hour of your time and undivided attention once a month during the coming year, the activity involved to be chosen by him. This may not sound like much, but how many of us really give any one child a piece of ourselves which he does not have to share with any other family member? It might do wonders for the generation gap or a broken-down relationship.

Well, we've only scratched the surface, but somehow it seems important in these days of ecology and conservation that our gifts be fewer and more meaningful, that we teach our children even affection is not to be squandered, that to mine the possibilities of one object is better than to flounder in extravagance and appreciate nothing.

The old-fashioned Christmas of an orange and a pair of hand-knit mittens was pretty Spartan, but we have traveled a long way in the other direction—too far perhaps. Maybe even the kids would enjoy less of an extravaganza and more of our honest attention. It's worth a try.

Mum's the Word

Kay slipped through my screen door, dropped wearily into a kitchen chair, and helped herself to an orange.

"That Jimmy," she sputtered. "I should have named him Trouble. He just goes from one disaster to another."

Visions of her ten-year-old barreled across my mind, his mischievous brown eyes peeping out from an undisciplined shock of blond hair, freckles spilling over the golden tan of fair skin. His shy, sweet smile had brightened my backyard activities many a morning. Now Kay threatened our fragile relationship with her disparaging word picture. Jimmy would never look quite the same to me again.

Why do we betray our children by parading their flaws before anyone who will listen?

The mother of a slow learner often feels impelled, when complimented upon the child's sunny disposition, to add, "but he has *such* a time in school." Why? Isn't it enough that he's the gentle peacemaker of the home? Must he be everything?

"Your Sara seems so problem free," comments a friend.

Mum's the Word

"You haven't seen her room," I reply, laughing. A little joke between mothers. But my friend will now always visualize our poised teenager against a backdrop of unmade beds and cluttered closets. Sara's housekeeping will improve. Why mess up the record with trivia?

We love, indulge, nurture our children, then use them to fill the gaps in dinner-party conversation. We may not do it maliciously, but we rob them of their dignity, their individual charms, before our friends.

Lately I've been assessing our offspring more positively. Our eldest son, now 15, has a few flaws obvious to his family, but the neighbors are charmed with his warm smile and outgoing personality. Is it necessary that they share the details of all his growing pains? Of course not!

At a recent parent-teacher conference where I received a glowing account of our youngest's virtues, I found myself with some negative comments teetering upon the tongue—a polite balancing of the ledger. But, no. She *is* all that the teacher said—thoughtful, kind, sensitive. Her faults, so minor, aren't public information.

Children in their sensitivity seldom knife us with betrayal. I have been amazed and grateful at the opportunities ours have bypassed to expose some shoddy aspect of parental natures. They may nick us with an amused glance or a sly wink, but no mirthful description of our vices is splattered abroad for the entertainment of our mutual friends. Certainly we must attempt to match that loyalty.

It takes special vision to sift out the blundering awkwardness of youth, leaving only the distillation of tenderness, whimsy, and curiosity which is a child. When the little one says good night, fresh from the tub and rich with kisses, it is not difficult to assess the jewel we possess. Next morning, however, torn jeans or rebellious words can blow this image all apart. Are we wise enough to shield their growing, their experimenting, their failures, with the protecting screen of our love?

Are we mature enough to see beyond the discipline problems, the carelessness, the clumsiness, to the adulthood toward which they strain?

So far, we have watched the full maturing of only one of our children. Sadly, I must admit that we too often complicated her small failures with the usual clichés and, worse yet, shared them with the neighbors.

"I hate to think what kind of housekeeper she'll be."

"She'll never get far in life with that attitude."

"That child will never know the value of a dollar."

"Etc. Etc."

Today our potential "failure" handles the roles of wife, mother, student, and career woman with finesse. What happened to the child who lost her shoes, squandered her money, and defended her theories a bit too vigorously? She learned by trial and error, her own innate good taste, and (I hope) by parental example to build her personal life-style. I hear myself expounding shamelessly upon her successes these days. Too bad she had to prove it all point by point before we dared believe.

They're pretty wonderful, these kids of ours. Let's not sell them short.

Three Suggestions for Raising Teenagers— No Guarantee

I had this chapter all written. I had entitled it "How to Raise a Teenager." After all, we have four in various stages of development, and I felt reasonably qualified.

Then suddenly there were two or three days when the generation gap, usually little more than a crevice in our home, became a canyon. Communication faltered about a once-friendly table.

It passed. We settled our matters of contention, though not wholly to anyone's satisfaction. The long process of forsaking childhood lurched uncertainly down the time-worn path once more, leaving mother chagrined and thoughtful. Such episodes had occurred before and would again. The yellow legal pad with its pompous, scribbled column lay mockingly upon my desk. How to Raise a Teenager, indeed!

So I started all over again. A new title: "Three Suggestions for Raising Teenagers—No Guarantee."

Suggestion No. 1: *Don't throw up your hands—the game's not over yet.*

Not long ago I was voicing all my fears and frustrations over one of our offspring to a pastor, a friend of many years. "I'm afraid he's setting the patterns for a lifetime," I fretted nervously.

He watched the youth under discussion bicycling lazily about the driveway and said calmly, "It's too soon to tell." He then added, "Suppose the world had judged our eventual worth by our sixteen-year-old outlook." He had made his point well—neither of us had had great ambitions or spiritual strength during our teens.

It's a temptation sometimes to say, "You're just never going to amount to anything," but do we have the prerogative? Do we know? My pastor-friend was right. At sixteen it is too soon to tell.

Suggestion No. 2: *Don't think your teenager must always be cheerful.*

We appreciate consistency and pay a friend a high compliment when we say, "She's always the same." But teenagers are *not* always the same. You can suggest to your daughter that her jeans are a bit shabby and she should relegate them to the trash. One day she will receive your advice and respond graciously; the next day the same suggestion may expose you to a tirade. No one wears *new* jeans. It takes months to get them to an acceptable state of deterioration. Do you want people to think she has nothing on her mind but clothes?

Boys when unhappy have a frightening way of gunning a motorcycle cross-lots over the lawn and down the road as though they could outdistance all misery by the thrust of a throttle.

Girls disappear, sullen and uncommunicative, into their rooms. Hours pass. About the time you think they've climbed out the window and forsaken home forever, they emerge cheerful and cooperative, offering to help with dinner preparations.

We wonder what happened to the pleasant child who gladdened us with kisses and lived only to please his mommy. Nothing really, I suppose. He's only trying to fight his way free from the apron strings, to gather up his courage for that leap into the adult world, ready or not. Some days it's unbearably hard, and he must find some excuse for disliking us a bit if he's ever to make the break. He needs to know we're whistling in the kitchen, not unduly alarmed by the acrobatics of his personality.

Suggestion No. 3: *Begin to let go.*

It's tempting to go on parenting, protecting, saying No, but there comes a time when we must trust what we have created. We must permit some decisions and some mistakes. The son of one of my friends said it very simply and eloquently. He had been telling his mother of the trips about the country he planned to make the moment he obtained his driver's license. He would drift south, work a bit, then head west. His eyes glowed at the prospect, and already his cape of freedom whipped eloquently in the wind. My friend looked at this dark-haired boy, so anxious to leave the protection of home, and wasn't at all sure she was ready.

"What's the hurry?" she asked, attempting the light touch. "I would worry a lot about you."

93

Where Are We Running?

He sobered and just for a moment the accumulated love of seventeen years hung fragile and sweet between them.

Then, smiling, he said gently, "I have to get free of you sometime, you know."

Not every teenager has that much insight. Perhaps when the time comes he will not go. Perhaps the dream will have been enough. But, at any rate, we must recognize that our children need to break gradually from our care.

In his preface to *Between Parent and Teenager,* Haim Ginott says it beautifully: "As parents, our need is to be needed; as teenagers their need is not to need us. This conflict is real; we experience it daily as we help those we love become independent of us.

"This can be our finest hour. To let go when we want to hold on requires utmost generosity and love. Only parents are capable of such painful greatness."

Theories on Teenagers

We have four teenagers in our home at the moment, and often they rebel, or at best smile, at the way of life we want for them. They are restless. Even if they were alone in their unrest, I would be frantic (sometimes I am anyway), but all about me I see troubled, searching youth. Ours are not alone. When parents meet, instead of talking about their work, their joy in Christ, or their hobbies, they talk of their children, their fears for them, their bewilderment.

"What did we do wrong?" "How do you solve the car problem?" "She won't accept a word of advice." "He never tells me where he's been or what he's planning." "We just found out our Nancy's been on drugs for months."

To some extent, of course, this problem has always been around. Breaking away from the security of home has never been easy, but somehow there seems to be more hostility in the process than in my generation. We secretly smiled at the absurdities of our elders and made definite plans for setting the world straight when our time came, but we were somehow less willing to hurt those with whom we'd spent our childhood.

So what's with our kids today? I suppose it's quite possible we've made some errors in raising them, but didn't our parents make errors too? Most of the parents with whom I compare notes weren't permissive; so we can't dismiss the entire problem with that popular excuse.

I have some theories—that's all they are, so take them or leave them.

No. 1. Everything comes too easy. Food, shelter, and clothing are available in abundance. One's status is measured by the brand of sneakers he wears, and shame on the mother who dares suggest a cheap but long-wearing variety.

In the day when a seventeen-year-old knew the family's security hung on his willingness to harvest wheat, peddle papers, or find a part-time job after school, a boy squared his shoulders and knew his own worth. There was a reason for existence. Because housewifely activities consumed so many hours, young girls knew their mothers simply couldn't handle it alone. At seventeen a girl baked bread, knew every phase of child care and all the horrors of house-cleaning. With the conveniences of the 70s she considers her mother's requests just so much "busywork."

We cannot go back, and I for one don't care to, but I do believe our culture contributes an aimlessness to our children's existence which we need to consider.

No. 2. Young people used to marry in their teens and

were usually about the serious business of life by the time they were twenty. They went from the economic struggle of their parental home to the economic struggle of their own home.

Today we urge, sometimes compel, our youth to acquire an education, and "please don't get married until you finish." Many times they aren't motivated to learn, have no idea what they want from life, and thus fritter away our money and their time.

No. 3. We offer them few heroes. The great men of integrity and high moral standards are historical figures—too dusty for today's youth. Hypocrisy in national leadership causes our teenagers to look upon adult authority figures with a skeptical eye. Is *anyone* for real? As Christian parents many of us have attempted to set a good example, but unfortunately the teenager isn't inclined to look to his parents as a pattern. (That comes later, often when he becomes a parent himself.) He does need a model, however, and too many times, for lack of anything better, he chooses a rock star, a sports hero, or the tough guy down the street.

Those are my theories. Where are my solutions? I really don't have any. We can't change the contemporary world. We can't insist that our children live frugally amid our affluence. We can't marry them off at eighteen. It *is* important to acquire some type of education. And we *are* pretty short on models of integrity.

The obvious, of course, is to introduce them to Jesus Christ, as the expression goes. I'm gradually coming to the conclusion, however, that one rarely *introduces* a teenager to Jesus if he's been raised in a Christian home. He's been nurtured on the conventional approaches. He's deaf to the jargon of conversion. Often, therefore, he must *find* Christ for himself, stumble upon Him as fresh and new as the young fishermen found Him beside the Sea of Galilee.

We can only ready them for that moment with our love and understanding, and we can pray that when the young Christ comes walking out of the morning mists toward our particular son or daughter, saying, "Follow Me," they'll see in Him all the wonder and the joy which has sustained us through the years.

How to Survive in a Houseful of Teenagers

A group of mothers sat behind a wall of glass at the local "Y" watching their offspring learn to swim. Just before the session ended, a career mother came rushing in. She had requested a few minutes from work to come and watch her five-year-old's progress. Her son did not expect her and so did not bother to glance often at the viewing window as did those whose mothers were there. He splashed awkwardly along the length of the pool, straining as he neared the end, but successful.

When he dripped wearily over the side, the other women knocked on the glass to attract his attention. As his mom was in the back row, he did not see her at once and, looking puzzled, started to turn away. The mothers all rapped again and pointed over their shoulders toward his pretty young parent.

Bewildered, his eyes searched the faces behind the glass once more, coming to rest at last upon that familiar figure waving proudly from the back. His face slid from disbelief to astonishment, then to utter radiance. Silence fell over the women, the mother in each of them responding to that unfeigned joy. Finally, into the stillness, one woman spoke softly, "My seventeen-year-old *used to* look at *me* like that."

The spell was broken. Everyone chuckled. Most of them knew from hard experience that a seventeen-year-old isn't usually swept off his feet by Mom's unexpected appearance. But we long to hold onto that blind adoration. It feels so good to have someone who thinks we're marvelous twenty-four hours a day.

However, somewhere along in the early teens the relationship begins to disintegrate. He no longer hangs on our every word nor considers our decisions pontifical. His personality seems to crack and heave as if at the mercy of an emotional volcano. All his weaknesses, evident off and on since birth, flash with frightening clarity through his days.

Yet, on the other hand, he often exhibits an amazing sensitivity and gentleness. He may be intensely creative. His concern for those outside the home can amaze you, in view of his seeming indifference to the feelings of his family. It's almost like being born all over again—this slow, agonizing emergence of the adult from the womb of childhood. It's painful, like any birth, for parent and child alike.

But just as we walked the floor at night with a wailing infant, not always sure of just what to do, so we must help with this new process. When a toddler is learning to walk, we do not go behind him all day, hands beneath his arms, supervising every inch of progress. We let him get up and fall down, get up and fall down, get up and fall down, interfering only with a hug and comfort when it all gets too discouraging or painful. We understand there's no easy way to emerge out of infancy.

Unfortunately, we are not that wise fifteen years later. We tend to meddle, to steer, to insist the adolescent conform to our mold. To some degree, he needs to sort out life on his own. A friend who has led his family of four quite successfully through the teens said, "When each child reached thirteen, we felt we had done about all we could in the matter of training him. From that point on we were just there when he needed us. If he squandered his earnings recklessly, we did not preach long sermons on thrift, but neither did we offer a loan when difficulties arose. We let life teach the lessons."

If we have been "hover mothers," it's time to back off. Teenagers hate reminders about jackets and vitamins. They are amazingly hardy (all that good care from babyhood!) and do not seem to contract pneumonia even under the most teeth-chattering conditions. There will be times, of course, when counsel is necessary, and thus it's important not to have done so much nagging over nonessentials that the victim has tuned us out completely.

There are instances when it's necessary to ask ourselves if the child is being rude or if we are being supersensitive. Often after visiting a home lush with drapes and carpeting, our teenagers tell us, "It sure would be nice to have a fancy place like that." Well, though I recognize the beauty of such a home, it so happens that I prefer the cozy look of braided rugs and ruffled white curtains.

Thus their implication that if we had more money or if I had better taste we could look like Mrs. Shag-rug always raises my hackles a bit. I find it necessary to remind myself over and over again that the child has a right to his own opinions, that it's quite normal for him to choose a life-style at variance with mine. It is part of his emancipation. So, ignoring my bruised ego, I determine to be thankful it is only my decorating talents he is rejecting rather than my moral values. As parents, we cannot allow ourselves the luxury of overreacting or becoming touchy.

The parent of teenagers should never cut himself off from friends and activities outside the home. After a heavy dose of "Now, Mother, you're being hopelessly old-fashioned," or "Dad, there's no use trying to talk to you; you never understand anything," the parent begins to experience a morbid sense of failure, not only as a parent but as a human being.

It becomes essential then to disassociate oneself temporarily from the home situation. An evening spent in adult company usually restores one's sanity and sense of self-worth. Home events fall into perspective. Dad and Mom may even bring themselves to chuckle over their problems on the way home. Just as teenagers need occasionally to escape our concern and supervision, so we need to escape their criticism and scorn. Any reminder that we are coping efficiently in the real world is good therapy.

It's also well to have an area of achievement to which the adult can turn when the arrogance of youth has eroded one's self-respect. To lose ourselves for an hour or two in some creative hobby or demanding activity at which we excel, restores our self-confidence and frees us to be more objective about our offspring's growing process. The teenager, though he may never admit it, takes pride in a parent who makes his mark in even a small way. He does not really want us just to build a tiny world about him and his activities but to have interests, dreams, and successes of our own.

We do, however, need to maintain an interest in what's going on with him, even at times to join him in some activity. Our youngest son has ridden motorcycles for years, as do most of his buddies. His best friend has become involved in cycle racing, and Mitch often goes to watch him compete. Several times he has urged us to join him. It hardly seems our kind of thing, but he asks so little of us that we set aside a Sunday afternoon to "watch Ronny race." Out on a wooded hillside, along with Ronny's parents—who happen to be our neighbors—we settled on a blanket, with lunch and cold drinks alongside, to view the dusty track.

I learned first of all that the rough atmosphere I had expected was nonexistent. It was mostly families watching their teenagers work off their excess energies on motorcycles. Accidents, they told me, were rare and seldom serious. And I found when Ronny raced, this youngster I had watched grow up with my own son, that I could hardly contain myself. I willed him around the curves and cheered proudly with his mom when he won. It still wasn't exactly my kind of thing, but I could understand my son's pleasure in being there and could honestly tell him I'd had fun. I could also stop worrying, for in seeing the event for myself, I'd been assured it was a harmless place for him to be on a Sunday afternoon.

My husband has now bought a motorcycle, and in a few months, when Mitch turns sixteen, they'll head out onto the highway together. Yes, I shall worry, but I must weigh the joy they will find in a shared interest against the physical dangers.

It wouldn't hurt to invite them occasionally into our world also. Now and then our children attend coin shows with their father and speaking engagements with me. It's not their thing either, but they come along anyhow and understand a bit more about those two mysterious people, their parents.

I have no idea what our last five children will do with their lives (the first has already grown and left us). I know only that we have loved them—sometimes wisely, sometimes not so wisely. They've forced us to live at levels of joy and pain we'd have never known without them. We've shared warm, happy days and bitter, hurting days. We've tasted life as it came to us. We're bound together by the fierce, strong ties of family. I dare to hope those ties will hold. We will not ask that they be carbon copies of us, their parents. Instead, we'll live wider and more interesting lives through their expanding worlds. And maybe— just maybe—they'll find in us something worthy of their exploration and respect.

Thoughts on Losing a Son

September has robbed me, and now she's trying to make amends with red vines on stone walls. Such charms, I must admit, do compensate to some small degree for my loss, but it's with a heavy heart I tramp her stubbled fields.

A week ago we took our eldest son away to boarding academy. With joy we had purchased new clothes, rugs, bedspread, blankets, sheets, towels, wastebasket, drapes —even a pencil sharpener.

With him we weathered out the registration lines, the schedule-planning lines, and the work assignment sector. Together we settled his room, and, as I made up his bed with brand-new sheets, some brand-new emotions began to inflict themselves, all uninvited, upon me.

Out in the hall I heard very casual farewells going on. I must swallow this lump in my throat and get on with the bed making. I'm always too emotional. We stored small items in drawers, large ones in cupboards, hung familiar clothes in an unfamiliar closet. We puttered and made small talk until there was nothing left with which to putter.

At which point our six-foot son, with his spanking-fresh driver's license, said, very offhandedly, "You'll have to keep an eye on the gas gauge, Mom. I won't be there to fill it up for you."

And I said, "You know I'll never remember." That was our farewell. (Now I understood the casual good-byes in the hall.) My heart stomped its feet and screamed, "I cannot take this," but my lips smiled and said inconsequentials.

Boots with a metal tap on the heel that always told me when he was around, maroon bell-bottoms with a tiny mend on the back pocket, white even teeth in a smile that had warmed our hearts for sixteen years, black collar-length hair shaped naturally to the head. I would tuck the picture away in my heart, for he'd never be quite the same again. In the independence of dormitory life youth achieves a self-sufficiency which snaps the apron strings abruptly. When we met again, self-confidence would have replaced the wistfulness in his eyes.

On the way home we treated the younger children to milk shakes, filled our back seat with apples and peaches from one of the many fruit stands along the way, and everything was normal, except my heart which ached and my ears which kept listening for the missing voice, the absent laughter. I wondered, riding along, how God said good-bye to *His* Son during those last moments together before Christ took off the shining robes of royalty and became one of us. I wonder what emotions surged through the heart of eternal God as He looked for the last time upon His *only* Son (I had others). Did They touch each other in farewell, or did They fear, as did I, that the moment was too fragile? One of my favorite writers penned these words: "It was a struggle, even for the God of the universe, to give up His Son." If so, did He too bow broken and sorrowing as He watched the manger drama unfold on Planet Earth, knowing it had to be, wanting it to be, but unable to silence His father-heart?

In the wonderful book *The Desire of Ages,* page 49, there are two paragraphs which suddenly mean a great deal more to me. Let me share them with you. "Satan in heaven had hated Christ for His position in the courts of God. He hated Him the more when he himself was dethroned. He hated Him who pledged Himself to redeem a race of sinners. Yet into the world where Satan claimed dominion God permitted His Son to come, a helpless babe, subject to the weakness of humanity. He permitted Him to meet life's peril in common with every human soul, to fight the battle as every child of humanity must fight it, at the risk of failure and eternal loss.

"The heart of the human father yearns over his son. He looks into the face of his little child, and trembles at the thought of life's peril. He longs to shield his dear one from Satan's power, to hold him back from temptation and conflict. To meet a bitterer conflict and a more fearful risk, God gave His only-begotten Son, that the path of life might be made sure for our little ones. 'Herein is love.' Wonder, O heavens! and be astonished, O earth!"

Blizzard

"My exams are over. I can come home for the weekend. Will you come and get me?"

"You were home just last weekend, Son. You know the school frowns on anything oftener than three weeks."

"I have permission already. *Please*."

"Mitch, it's a long drive down there, and the weather's bad. I think you should stay put until your regular leave." I was puzzled. This boy rarely made unreasonable requests and never pursued them stubbornly.

"Ask Dad. Maybe *he'll* come and get me."

Persistence triumphed. Dad headed that night for the boarding academy eighty miles away. Four hours later father and son were safely home.

Next morning daughter Amy, thirteen, boarded the bus at 7:00 AM for the city of Rochester thirty-five miles away, where she attends a private Christian school. Snow swirled about the back door as she left.

"Come home at noon if it gets too bad," I called.

Two hours later she phoned from the bus stop. "Come and pick me up. Please, Mom. When I got into Rochester, it was snowing so hard, I just hopped another bus and came home.''

"Well, honey," I chided, "why did you do that? You should have at least gone to school until noon to get your assignments.''

"I don't know," she defended lamely. "I just couldn't decide what to do.''

I pursued it no further, for she wasn't the school-skipping kind. But I was perplexed. She had braved many fiercer days in her years of commuting.

Our pastor called, reporting Mitch's school had closed for two weeks due to the natural gas shortage.

Along about noon, very suddenly as if someone had flipped a switch, the wind began screaming over the earth, whipping the light snow which had fallen all morning into blinding curtains of swirling white before the eyes of bewildered motorists. Traffic came to an abrupt halt, cars scattering about dangerously on the highways. We could not see our big red barn from the house. How would my husband ever get home from work? I went to the phone, only to find the circuits so jammed that calls were impossible. By nightfall we knew he would spend the night at his office like thousands of other western New Yorkers. Radio and television emitted unnerving warnings: *Do not leave your home for any reason. Zero visibility. Heavy drifting. All roads closed.*

It was Friday night—family night—the Sabbath. We gathered, the children and I, about the fireplace, uneasy without the head of our household and wondering when the power lines would snap in the forty-five-mile-an-hour gale.

"Do you know, Mom, where I would have been when the storm hit, if I hadn't come home?" Amy asked.

I hesitated a moment, thinking. "Downtown Rochester at the bus terminal," I gasped, my heart thumping at the thought: a thirteen-year-old girl trapped with strangers in that public place for who knows how long.

"And while we're on that subject," Mitch said, "if I hadn't come home last night, I'd have been stranded at school when it closed."

At that moment my simple morning prayers for the children's safety took on fresh meaning. "Well, my children," I told them, "God brought everyone home but Daddy. Suppose He has that arranged too?"

At eleven o'clock we banked the fire, said our good nights, and listened to the shrieking winds from the luxury of warm beds. Sleep had just dragged me down into that cozy black pit from which one returns only with great effort, when the stairway light clicked on and to my sleepily astonished vision appeared God's last gift of the day, my husband.

"There seemed to be a brief lull in this mess; so I decided to give it a try. Made it to the neighbor's yard and hoofed it from there." He shivered, shaking snow from his coat.

The storm roared on for two days, but this family, which had learned new lessons in God's concern for His children, relaxed and enjoyed its togetherness.

Try These Tips for Better Living

Seventh-day Adventists are concerned with matters of health. Formerly, our friends have been amused but tolerant—our critics just amused. Suddenly, however, *everyone* is concerned with health and we aren't so lonely anymore. (Entire books have been written on why Seventh-day Adventists take health so seriously, but briefly we believe the body to be the temple of God [1 Corinthians 3:16, 17] and have also found it very difficult to practice the Christian virtues with a headache.) So I'll share with you a few health tips while they are in fashion.

Instead of the usual breakfast cereals, many of which are low in nutrients and high in preservatives, try the following (your only problem will arise in keeping it on hand, for children love it either in place of, or on top of, their usual morning cereal):

Granola

7 cups oatmeal (uncooked)
1 cup wheat germ

1 cup coconut
½ cup brown sugar
  or honey
½ cup oil
½ cup water
1 tablespoon vanilla
1 teaspoon salt
1 cup slivered almonds
½ cup pecans, whole

Mix ingredients thoroughly, and bake in shallow pans at 275°F until coconut is lightly browned—approximately one hour. Add diced dates in quantity desired and store in refrigerator.

Most Seventh-day Adventists are vegetarians. We long ago decided that the diet God prescribed for Adam and Eve (Genesis 1:29) was good enough for us. Besides, killing, even of animals, seems a strange act. Thus over the years we've developed many meatless recipes, some with the aid of commercial meat substitutes, some without. The following requires only ingredients readily available to any housewife.

Meatballs

Grind fine:
¼ cup cheese
1 onion
¼ cup walnuts
9 soda crackers

Try These Tips for Better Living

Season to taste with salt, sage, nutmeg, garlic, and chili powder. Add two eggs (more or less depending upon size of eggs), shape into small balls, brown in oil, and simmer in tomato sauce. Serve as entrée or with spaghetti. Serves two or three.

Get seven or eight hours of rest each night. This is a tough one for me, because I begrudge time spent in sleep, yet if I'm to appreciate the joys of the day, it's a necessary evil. I've learned from hard experience that the fruits of five- and six-hour nights are depression, irritability, lack of enthusiasm, and inability to contribute much to those about me. So early to bed. Ugh!

Try to get some outdoor exercise each day. It will have to be something more interesting than deep knee bends before an open window or all one's good resolutions will fall by the way. Last spring Don and I purchased bicycles and rediscovered the cherry-blossom magic of a country road on April mornings. At 7:15, the children already deposited upon the school bus, we mount our shining, multispeed vehicles and coast down our driveway into a green, invigorating world I'd forgotten existed. Don, who cannot do things in halfway measure, soon leaves me far behind.

I discover both hills and muscles I am unaware of, but there are compensations too. The day loses, as it moves along, something which is there at early morning, something which I had not experienced since the two-mile hike to a one-room Vermont schoolhouse nearly forty years before. The air seems guaranteed to restore youth, while the eye feasts on wild strawberry blossoms unfolding among the stones at road's edge. Small farm ponds wink and shimmer against a backdrop of cowslips. Suddenly I am "no age" but simply part of this great sprawling creation which has tumbled out of God's hand. Those aching leg muscles aren't even me. I'm cardinal call and trillium and gratitude.

If you can't bicycle, walk. It will do just as well. Make it a habit to bring something home with you—a leaf, a stone, a feather, or a flower. The search for "a lovely" is elixir for the mind.

Life is good and should be enjoyed in peak condition. Cast your personal vote for better health. I'll be thinking about you while I'm gasping over the crest of that last long hill.

Menu for a Cold Winter Night

When a late afternoon blizzard hurls itself down the valley, locking our old white farmhouse in its own private world of dancing flakes, I rejoice. I pretend that the stand of evergreens beyond our living-room windows stretches on and on, an endless forest, that we are alone in some winter wilderness. We stack apple logs beside the blazing fireplace and go often to the windows to dream into the soft, swirling dusk. Birds gather at the feeder, feathers puffed against the long, cold night. I indulge a fanciful daydream about bringing them in and lining them up along the windowsills to share our warmth. Tiny cups filled with sunflower seeds and suet would be a proper menu, I decide.

And speaking of eating, a night like this deserves a special meal. I admit, with some reluctance, that I don't like to cook, but if I must waste my time in such activity, I want the results to merit the effort; so I have gathered a dependable and tasty collection of recipes from magazines, cookbooks, and friends.

We do our eating on a remodeled sun porch where we

can look out into the blizzard from our snug window-walled retreat. It makes everything taste better. Now, on this stormy night, I've decided to share with you my menu. Maybe someday, when sleet tatoos *your* window, you'll like to try it too.

Elvira's potato pot

(I have yet to meet the person who doesn't like this dish.)

  6-8 medium potatoes cooked, cooled, peeled, and shredded
    2 cups shredded Cheddar cheese
   ¼ cup melted butter
    2 cups sour cream
   ⅓ cup chopped green onions (use some of the tops for color)
  1¼ teaspoon salt

Mix all ingredients. Bake in 9″ × 13″ pan at 350°F for 30-40 minutes until golden and slightly crispy on edges.

Cottage cheese loaf

½ cup margarine
1 cup chopped onion
1 cup chopped pecans
3 teaspoons chicken seasoning
1 package George Washington Seasoning and Broth

6 eggs
½ cup milk
1 quart cottage cheese
3½ cups Special K
1 13-ounce can Soya-meat (chicken style)

Menu for a Cold Winter Night

Sauté onion, pecans, chicken seasoning, and broth powder in margarine. Beat eggs and milk together and combine with diced Soyameat and remaining ingredients. Bake in well-greased, large, flat pan in 350°F oven for 1½ hours. Top will be dark brown when finished baking.

Remember, many of us are vegetarians, so there is no meat in the above loaf, but it is high in protein. You will find it delicious. If you can't locate on your supermarket shelves the meat substitute listed, it can be omitted from the recipe without changing the final product to any great extent.

Tropical green salad

(This is my own invention. It's pretty and different.)

Wash, dry, and tear one head of lettuce and a half bag of spinach.

Add slivers of green pepper and cucumber sliced very thin.

Add one can mandarin oranges, chilled and drained.

Toss with your favorite dressing.

I am going to use buttered carrots for this meal. This vegetable is one of my favorites, and it adds a lot of color to the menu.

Joyce Schnell's pistachio pudding

Prepare two packages of Pistachio Instant Pudding, using ½ cup less milk than called for on box. Add one

9-ounce container of Cool Whip and one can crushed pineapple, drained. This pudding can be served as is, topped with whipped cream or chopped pistachios, or it can be served over a simple cake.

Here Comes Your Plane Now, Chris

This afternoon I put our six-year-old grandson on the plane to fly across the country to his parents' home in San Francisco. As he, very tiny in his new red Snoopy suit, trudged beside the stewardess up the steps to the plane I was filled with respect for his courage.

On the way to the airport he'd said, in his open, trusting way, "It's all right to be a little bit afraid when you fly, isn't it, Grandma?"

I assured him that I was filled with a heady mixture of terror and excitement every time I took to the skies.

Fifteen minutes later, waiting to board and dancing with anticipation, he'd announced he was going to be a pilot when he grew up. I noted a healthy sense of adventure had infiltrated his uneasiness.

It occurred to me that in almost any new undertaking it's OK to be "a little bit afraid." In fact, anyone with good sense considers the possibility of mishap or failure. I never walk onto a platform to fulfill a speaking engagement without mixed emotions. Looking out across the faces of the audience, I'm challenged and excited with the opportunity to share that which is important to me. I'm also keenly aware that it's possible to lose one's chain of thought, or worse yet, the attention of the audience. *Most opportunities are embroidered with risk.*

It's that "little bit of fear" which prompts us to give it our best, to prepare thoroughly, and for me, at least, to put my trust in God and not in myself.

When we called San Francisco tonight to see how our young traveler had fared, confidence reigned. He had conquered the skies with his "little bit of fear" in his pocket where it belonged. I have no concern for his future.

I treasure another memory of his visit with us. This city-bred boy loves to tramp about in the fields and woods; so on Sabbath afternoon his grandfather and I took him on a long hike. Eventually his grandfather disappeared. Then he called for us to follow, through a scraggle of underbrush, to where he sat by a small hidden pond, fed by a whispery waterfall.

To reach the spot, one of *my* height must bend nearly double beneath the overhanging greenery while navigating, underfoot, a narrow, slippery area along the stream bed. I'm afraid I sighed . . . right out loud. Next thing, Grandfather would be inviting us down a rabbit hole!

Sensing my lack of enthusiasm, Christopher grinned up at me, reached out a small perspiring hand and encouraged, "Follow me, Grandma. I'll get you there."

Then, as I scroonched along behind him, I heard him mutter, "Boy, I sure hope I know where I'm going."

My insect bites, scratches, and wet feet were forgotten. I had a good chuckle to myself. He had spoken for us all. How often we call, "Follow me," while inwardly searching for the next foothold. He might have said, "I don't see how Grandpa got in there. Let's sit here and wait for him," but this little guy, who knew a lot more about cable cars, freeways, and condominiums than his present muddy predicament, forged ahead and arrived very shortly at his destination. We sat by the tiny pool, listening to the waterfall a long time.

Lead on, Christopher. I may not always be able to follow, but I shall watch your progress with interest and a great deal of love.

Did She Miss Him?

Amy, our youngest, had wheedled us into attending the local fair. All her teenage brothers and sisters had come and gone as they pleased throughout the week, and I well understood the longing in those brown eyes as it came down to the final days. I, too, had loved the fair as a little girl. So we ate a hasty supper and set off to see the sights.

Husband Don idled patiently while Amy and I inspected the baked goods, flower arrangements, and needlework displays. Looking at prizewinning vegetables, now comically withered beneath their blue ribbons, we chuckled and said to each other, "Got better cucumbers than that right home in our own garden."

Then we strolled down to the animal pens especially to see the chickens, for chickens were our latest venture into farming. By this time it was getting dark, and after a thorough inspection of every imaginable fowl, Amy urged us to get on to livelier things.

At age eleven I, too, had been drawn by the colorful honky-tonk of the midway, but at forty-seven I am possessed of a curious aversion to its noise and dirt. We had,

Did She Miss Him?

however, promised her a ride on the ferris wheel (and I do still enjoy that!); so we headed for the bright lights. Several rides, sugared waffles, and mirror-maze visits later, I sat on a bench in the darkness waiting while Amy rolled and somersaulted about in some sort of air-mattress bubble tent called the Moon Walk. Don had strolled off to watch thrill-hungry teenagers catapult into space on one of the more hair-raising rides.

I was alone—or almost alone. A few yards away the youth who sold tickets to the Moon Walk leaned on the back two legs of his chair against the tent. Fine blond hair fell over his forehead and onto his shoulders. A cigarette dangled loosely from his lips. There was about him an air of detachment, as though he had dismissed life as unworthy of his attention.

It suddenly hit me that he was very young—not much older perhaps than our youngest son, Mitch. It also occurred to me he probably had a mother. Did she miss him or worry about him? Was he ever a little boy, fresh and innocent and full of silly questions? If so, where had they gone? I tried to imagine *my* son far from home, drifting about the land, already old and bored, his eyes locked against his fellowmen. I was tempted to speak to the youth—to ask him where home was, if he had a family, and if he got some orange juice every day—but I lacked the courage to invade his shield of scorn.

All about me the carnival whirled on, but there in my dark corner, I looked up and was startled to find stars serene and detached in the night sky, glittering reminders

123

Where Are We Running?

that God was going calmly about His business of preparation for whatever events lie ahead.

Rock music throbbed over the general confusion of the midway. Humanity wandered from thrill to thrill, clutching cotton candy and spicy Polish sausages. Hard and lonely people reached out at us rural bumpkins with greedy hands. "Take a few shots at the ducks, mister. You're sure to win." "Let me guess your weight." "Win your girl a prize." "Three seats left for Bingo. Hurry, lady, game's about to start." All interspersed by the loudspeaker and the whine of racing cars at the grandstand.

Run, run, children of earth! Seek a new game, a new scare, a new taste sensation. Keep moving! For He seeks you, quietly, relentlessly, lovingly. Keep close to the rock group or the grandstand or the laughter of friends, else you'll hear Him calling, lonely in the night. And there's no resisting that voice.

Let yourself be flung up and over and upside down, round and round, till there's no sensation left to be discovered. But hurry on. Never stop. If you hesitate, if you are still, He will overtake you, and you will be drawn to Him, halted by His love, surrounded by His gentleness, and He will teach you a new way. Sometimes it's painful to learn a new way. It's only for the brave, for the seekers.

For you? I do not know. Only you can tell.

December

Today I am weary of causes and issues. I don't care whether I'm liberated or the victim of my womanhood.

I've had it with child-raising methods which never seem to work.

I'm emotionally numb from identifying with the starving thousands across the waters. How long can one's heart break over an endless, unsolvable tragedy?

I don't want to sew dresses for my daughters, nor dream up new themes for church programs.

Already I panic at the oncoming holidays. Gift list. Card list. Menus. Wrapping. Decorating. Mailing. Stretching dollars over last-minute unexpected gifts.

Deliver me, just today, from the clothes that must be dropped off at the cleaners and the grade card that must be discussed with a teacher.

Don't tell me about the drug problem nor offer me Dave Wilkerson's books.

I don't want to know that hundreds of college graduates can't find work nor that the economic structure in our country walks a tightrope.

Where Are We Running?

Today I do not wish to bear the burden of all my fellowmen who are indifferent to Jesus Christ. Don't show me the eager youth upon the streets who approach the stranger to ask whether he's saved.

Don't quote me politicians babbling peace as blithely as if the nations were their yo-yos. Neither read me headlines about Ishmael and Isaac's old, old war nor debate the moral aspects of abortion or euthanasia.

Leave me alone. Do not even ask me which kind of oven cleaner works the best, or what I shall prepare for dinner tonight.

I shall sit a bit here in our window-walled family room and watch the traffic at the bird feeder while the first powdery snow dusts bare maples. Six cardinals, flaming in a white birch, wait for blue jays to finish haggling over corn. Who made the rule that blue jays eat first? Do cardinals need liberating? There's a certain loveliness in their patient courtesy. Perhaps it's the blue jays that need liberating—from arrogance.

At the closer windowsill feeder, juncos and chickadees whiz in and out like commuters at a coffee shop. Fearless little funnies, they assume all men are friends. I wish to hold one in my hand and feel his tiny feet.

Upon the closest maple a downy woodpecker clings to the suet station created by son Mitchell. It is a simple wooden frame covered with chicken wire through which the suet fanciers help themselves to a feast.

I contemplate this son's ingenuity, his pleasure in such projects. He it is who brings in the black walnuts in the fall, wrestling them from their outer coverings with methods too irksome for the rest of us. His are the Scotch pinecones, collected sometimes from the very treetops, and sprayed gold for the holiday season. This boy suddenly comes into focus. He responds to beauty. He rises to a challenge. He'll be all right. In all my frantic bustlings I'd too often seen only his problems before.

I pray. Not hurriedly, with a dozen duties pressing in. I have dismissed duty for the day. I am still for a long time, no longer pouring out a frantic coverage of my worries and needs. I do not beg. For once I am quiet before God. I bow my head and let His thoughts come to me as they will, simply resting in His presence. A new experience. Asking no questions. Feeling no guilt. Demanding no solutions. Just being with Him.

Later, I walk through the snowy woods, praising God for specific small things. The jack-in-the-pulpit lying dormant beneath frozen soil. The red squirrel who scampers above me, sending down small blizzards upon my head. The promise of spring in buds already formed upon the twigs. For the fact that my eyes are not indifferent to beauty. I walk as Eve must have walked through Eden, savoring, grateful, wondering. The stillness of the woods matches the stillness of my soul. I do not feel uneasy about my temporary leave of absence from schedules, routine, and confusion. The King Himself has said, "Be still, and know that I am God" (Psalm 46:10). Most of the time this experience has to be snatched, a moment here, a moment there, from the scramble of living.

Where Are We Running?

Tomorrow, bring on hurt and concern, duty and experiment, failure and forgiveness, for today I've found a mending for my soul.